PAKISTAN
MANIFEST DESTINY

ATIF F QURESHI

epicpress

Pakistan
Manifest Destiny

An Epic Press book

Copyright © 2009 Atif F Qureshi

ISBN 978-0-9556570-0-9

A catalogue record of this book is
available from the British Library

Author online at *www.pakdestiny.net*

بســـــــم الله الرحمن الرحيـــــــم

Dedicated to my parents

PAKISTAN
MANIFEST DESTINY

"The world, but not self, thou canst see;
How long in thy ignorance wilt thou sit?
With thy ancient flame let the night be lit;
The hand of Moses is sleeved in thee!

Set forth thy foot from the circling skies;
Greater and older than these thou art;
Fearest thou death in thy deathless heart?
Death's but a prey that before thee lies!

Life, once given thee, none can take;
'Tis for lack of faith men faint and die;
Learn to be sculptor, even as I,
And haply anew thy self-hood make!"

Allama Iqbal

"In keeping silent about evil, in burying it so deep within us
that no sign of it appears on the surface, we are implanting it,
and it will rise up a thousand-fold in the future. When we
neither punish nor reproach evildoers... we are ripping the
foundations of justice from beneath new generations."

Alexander Solzehnitsyn

CONTENTS

PREFACE

"We are in the midst of unparalleled difficulties and untold sufferings; we have been through dark days of apprehension and anguish; but I can say with confidence that with courage and self-reliance and by the Grace of God, we shall emerge triumphant!"

Quaid-e-Azam

How, you ask, did it all begin? At first it was as an ache in the heart, a sigh. Then, a whisper: a desire to mould a destiny that would shape the lives of millions. From this glacial shift came an avalanche of protest that brought together saintly leaders who would re-write the face of history forever. Being the giants among men that they were, it was perhaps only too easy it seems for Allama Muhammad Iqbal and Muhammad Ali Jinnah to cast an inspired vision onto a map, and then with a thick red marker transform it into reality. It was with that red line that they sparked the revival of the entire Ummah.

It was a long time coming. With the rapid descent and decline of Islamic civilisations the world over, it had seemed that dawn would never break upon the darkness that consumed the Muslims. But Iqbal had awoken a sleeping nation, revitalising it with the energetic spirit of a profound spiritual destiny. Now each imagined themselves anew, in a land that echoed long gone halcyon days of faith and purity in mind and flesh. Millions were stirred by his bracing words: *"Arise and soar with sun's new-born rays, to breathe new life into dying nights and days!"*

It was a hint of something that had only been achieved in days of old, often told from pulpits and podiums across the land. Defining events from fourteen centuries ago that still seemed as fresh as if they had occurred only yesterday. What more could one ask for? To exist in a land where all around blossomed the fragrance of good, to live in secluded cleanliness, free from the dirt and grime of colonial shame? Invigorated by a beautiful ideology, a sense of hope infused millions of hearts.

Now, many decades later, as we look back on years of strife, division and poverty, cultivated by generations of villainous leaders, we find ourselves wondering how this glorious inheritance became so spoiled. Pakistan, in its early conception, carried with it a heavy burden of expectation, most of which has remained unfulfilled. But then, what did *we* ever do for Pakistan, apart from failing her at every turn, and carelessly tossing aside the precious legacy that our forefathers left us?

Even now, there is no doubt in my mind or in my heart that Pakistan is unique amongst the world's nations. She has the greatest potential for good and the greatest tendency toward nobility. Pakistan's time will soon come. Her destiny *is* manifest and when Allah wills it, she will stand upright as a shining beacon of hope for all mankind.

No doubt, the perils between us and the glorious Camelot we strive for are treacherous, but is that any reason for us to waver? Let us take a lesson from those generations of yesteryear who stood determined, and against the odds, struggled toward an unknown nation that to them was the repository of their hopes and aspirations. They ventured out undaunted towards that distant horizon - and so can we now.

Let us not be troubled or deterred by current travails. We must strive hard, ever forward, and insensitive to dangers. We still have time. Our nation is young. Her potential is boundless, limitless, a vista of infinite possibilities, each better than the next. Let there be no doubt or hesitation in our minds, for of one thing we can be certain - Allah did not create Pakistan in vain.

INTRODUCTION

"Why this retribution - where lies your fault? Poor little
bird! Can't you untie this knot? Regretfully, you could not
be an Eagle, since the hints of nature you noticed not."

Allama Iqbal

Pakistan's arrival onto the world stage was nothing short of
miraculous, a nation bursting into life through the sheer
force of divine providence. Foreseen in the vision of Allama
Iqbal and created with the perspiration of Mohammed Ali
Jinnah, the new nation was the fulfilment of a manifest destiny
- arising to defend the Ummah in her darkest hour. But in the
critical moments after independence, Pakistan was in difficult
territory. A land of subsistence farmers and struggling
immigrants, the nation's position was precarious and her long
term prospects were uncertain.

Yet even through those early days, even after the spilt blood,
the lost wealth, and the broken ties, there was a sense of
enormous anticipation. The Pakistani people were energised,
aspiring and free, daring to strike out into a bright future no
longer burdened by world war, religious insecurity or the shame
of subservience to foreign masters.

But the optimism soon turned to ashes. The great tragedy of
the Pakistani saga is the sense of frustration carried in the
hearts of its people today. The people of Pakistan love their
nation immensely, but they so richly deserve the Pakistan that
should have been. Instead, betrayed by fate, they now witness a

1

'terra incognita' - an unrecognisable land. Yet the potential of this wonderful nation with its warm, beautiful people is colossal. On paper it has every advantage: a hardworking entrepreneurial population, rich resources, and a forward thinking progressive attitude. Nevertheless, Pakistan has failed to live up to expectations.

For the affected in the midst of all the disquiet, coming to terms with this malaise is not easy. Considering they were once the standard bearers of a glorious Muslim civilisation, for the people of Pakistan, national decline and stagnation is a bitter pill to swallow. Debate and commentary is rife about the possible causes, and opinions are ten a penny. Truly or falsely, politicians, the Army, America, and countless other factors are cited for blame. But as Confucius once said, *"it is better to light one small candle than to curse the darkness,"* so let us illuminate the plain yet not so obvious truth. There is a factor in play that trumps all others in its capacity to make regret our past, misery our present, and despair our future. It is the entrenchment of *socialism*.

Socialism has been a dead weight around the neck of Pakistan. It has derailed her fate as Quaid-e-Azam envisioned to be *"one of the greatest nations of the world"*. Through its terrible effects, our collective hopes and aspirations have been humbled. The results of liberal socialism and heavy government interventionism have led to immense decay and stagnation in almost every aspect of national life. With problems now ranging from the breakup of the family unit to central bank instigated inflation, the failed policies of successive governments have crippled our beloved country. This can come as no surprise though, because socialism, being a man-made Western construct, inherently repudiates the principled Islamic values our ideological nation was founded on.

First, let us clearly define what socialism is: socialism is primarily rooted not in economic, but in cultural and social principles. It would be fair to call it an egalitarian creed because it places the notion of 'equality' above all others in all aspects of national life, an attractive proposition to the poverty stricken masses that would benefit most if socialism ever delivered. In order to restructure society along egalitarian lines, socialists espouse the creation of a powerful government that has control over a sizeable proportion of the wealth of the nation. This government owns, operates and interferes; imposing infrastructure and control which it seeks to fund by borrowing at interest, printing 'paper' money, and taxing industry and individuals. As funds flow from one source, they are redistributed elsewhere as the government chooses.

Tinkering with the economy is the main predilection. Industries that are deemed priorities are propped up, businesses are interfered with, and prices manipulated. But this clumsy government intervention disrupts market forces, creates havoc in the economy and retards economic growth. Normal, hardworking families struggle day to day burdened with unfair taxation and inflation and little prospect of decent education, health care or opportunities for employment. Meanwhile, the privileged few who have access to the corridors of power live lives far removed from those of the common man. Hardly unexpected, as socialism fosters corruption and nepotism on a prolific scale. It leads to the creation of a parasitic elite class who get ahead by influencing and leaching off the government to line their pockets at everyone else's expense.

All socialist economies have massive, inefficient public sector industries and departments full of people engaging in largely unproductive work. In effect, this absurd economic model allows the government to effectively buy off large swathes of the population by simply employing them. And when the State pretends to provide work, services or any bounty no matter how poor those provisions may be, the habits and actions of individuals and businesses are severely distorted. Worst of all, the State acquires a demigod-like status as the populace turn to it for all their worldly needs. Essential moral and spiritual values are compromised and forgotten - thus families and communities fracture.

Red tape and inane beaurocracy are the hallmark. With so many regulations and hoops to jump through to get anything done, incidences of bribery and corruption are multiplied. When opportunities to get ahead are so rare, desperate people turn to crime and disorder. The poor and the under-classes, who were conned into utopian illusions, are the most severely affected. With little opportunities for employment or advancement, the ladder of social mobility is kicked away. Price fixing, minimum wages and 'poverty alleviation' programmes each add to the crippling effects of economic mismanagement. For the poor, they do more harm than good. Poverty becomes entrenched and those born poor are entirely likely to stay that way. When life is so dependent on the State, there are few ways to escape.

We recognize this awful picture because apart from Pakistan, it also describes what many other nations have been reduced to, but the inevitable questions follow: where did this creed come from, and why are we burdened with it?

Contemporary socialism is essentially a European idea which originated in the 19th century. This was the so-called Romantic era which gave birth to many an unconventional philosophy. It was the age of Darwin, Wagner, Hegel, and of Karl Marx, a man who would have a profoundly disturbing influence on the fate of hundreds of millions. Although Marx and his associate Engels espoused socialism of a more extreme form, his political theories gave rise to the so-called revisionists and trade unionists whose 'social democratic' adaptation of socialism would have wide popular appeal - that is, to the ruin of many a nation.

In the early 20th century, the populist messages of the moderate socialist democratic and extremist Bolshevik parties resulted in the rise of socialism as a political force in Europe. Socialism took a firm foothold in the parliaments and dictatorships of the Western powers. The immediate results led to economic instability, boom-bust cycles and depressions. As a consequence of the economic chaos, fascist, ultra-nationalist movements arose in Europe which called for governments to reverse the economic gloom by further 'nationalising' the economy and spending heavily on aggressive militarism. Harnessing the industry and wealth that had been achieved by preceding generations, these nations then launched themselves with vigour into World Wars that would topple European hegemony forever.

After the turmoil and destruction of years of industrialised warfare, broken and exhausted, Britain forsook its imperial ambitions. In 1947, in the last throes of its superpowerdom, the British partitioned India and withdrew. Not without regret. India had been the apple of Britain's eyes; with Queen Victoria once regarding it *"the jewel in the crown"*. But a new chapter had opened in the many-thousand year history of the subcontinent. Formerly enslaved, now the subcontinent turned its attention to independence and freedom. Although marred by bloodletting, war and strife in the early years, its people gazed into a bright future of independent existence. But it was not to be. These fledgling nations had few ideas of their own. In the newly liberated colonies, the legacy of the West still had a stranglehold.

In spite of their physical freedom, both Pakistani and Indian leaders remained mentally shackled. Imperial Britain had passed on the torch to a well-trained cadre of 'brown sahib imperialists' who would take on the burden of rule. These former collaborators remained in thrall to their former masters and were unable to shake off deep rooted complexes about the West; it was a direction in which they constantly turned to for guidance. These new elite political classes, having been mis-educated at crème de la crème Western universities, had returned to their countries with minds overflowing with the most fashionable economic theories of the day. The latest economic credo in vogue at Oxford University and the London School of Economics were ill-thought through, populist dogmas of nationalisation, protectionism and social egalitarianism.

So although freed from the yoke of colonialism, and at liberty to create the classical Islamic economy that had worked such wonders during the 'Golden Era' of the early Caliphate, Pakistan instead stumbled into the economic travails of social democracy and 'interest-based inflationary capitalism'. To be fair, it was difficult to escape such a fate, and while only a brave and visionary leadership could have done so, there was none to be found.

The Pakistani political classes fell into lock step with the fashionable Western creed that was being implemented with zeal as the economic model of choice across the world. It was not pursued out of a sense of benevolence. For national leaders, socialism had enormous advantages, and they knew it; its populist ideas won more votes, increased spending meant more funds flowing through sticky fingers into Swiss bank accounts, and it allowed leaders to expand their influence in the economy and reward supporters with land, jobs and favours.

Corrupt leaders saw social democracy as an excellent way to wrest further control from their respective populations and entrench their power and influence into every aspect of national life. The creed of more government activity and intervention played perfectly into their hands. Decrees poured out of ministries regulating every activity ranging from business, culture to even family life. The simple freedom of the common man to go about his business and fulfil his God-given potential was crushed under the heel of petty beaurocrats. Propaganda gushed forth with ideas of the emancipation of the unprivileged classes while reality told a different story - the systematic oppression of the poor and underprivileged by the elite few in fortified positions of power.

While in the Far East, free markets were rapidly enriching formerly ravaged and war torn nations, short-sighted leaders in Pakistan remained unwilling to take the brave measures that would secure her future. It is a tragedy of colossal proportions. Even today, the current state of affairs leads any person of common sense to invariably question the system, ideology and leaders who have brought Pakistan to such a pitiful state. Social democracy has totally failed to live up to the required expectations of progress and growth. As long as Pakistan continues to pursue economic policies and objectives that ape Western socialism, there can be no hope.

The results are before us. Never mind the likes of South Korea, Malaysia and China who have raced far ahead, at the time of writing, the average Pakistani has approximately the same dollar income as the average Vietnamese citizen. Yes. Vietnam. The same Vietnam whose entire economy was annihilated in the 1960's by a merciless American war that left over 3 million dead, only to be followed by fifteen years of equally merciless communist rule, forced collectivisation and severe restrictions on private enterprise. While the Vietnamese leadership wisely abandoned socialism in 1986, our leaders stubbornly cling to it even today. The result: Vietnam now has one of the most open, dynamic and fastest growing economies in the world. Incredibly, in spite of the pain they have endured, over the last 20 years Vietnam has gone from virtually zero to already catching up to, if not surpassing Pakistan due to the vigour of their free enterprise system.

How much more proof do we need? The record is clear; history teaches us that socialism has never enabled a nation to break free of the chains of poverty. Yet after many decades of continual failure, why do we still assume that it will work for us? While misguided folk still fixate on 'Western social democracy', what they fail to grasp is that technologically advanced nations today that may be termed as 'welfare states' were not always so. Not a single one of the Western powers ever implemented socialist credo during their ascendance, i.e. during the transition from agrarianism to industrialisation. For these nations, socialism was never a vehicle for growth and modernisation. The Western powers are prosperous and powerful today, but not because of their current socialistic policies. The prosperity they now enjoy is, to a large extent, inherited. Westerners today benefit largely from the fruit of their ancestors efforts.

Their ancestors were advocates and practitioners of 'free enterprise', a system whereby free markets are allowed to allocate the factors of production in the most efficient manner possible without much interference from government. It was this that ushered in the 'industrial revolution' in Britain. Within a relatively short space of time, the reliance on free enterprise allowed this small, insignificant island nation to grow, industrialise and raise its living standards at a rate never before seen in history. Other European and North American nations followed suit and, as the East fell far behind, Western nations modernised fast. Western power thus expanded rapidly and by orders of magnitude. Their dynamic free market economies propelled social mobility, wealth creation, speculation, industrialisation and high commerce.

Economic prosperity raised living standards while swelling the coffers of Western treasuries giving these nations the confidence and resources to exert their influence far from home. So it was that colonies were won and Western imperialism was born. The strength and resources to export force, whether for good or evil, is built on the foundation of a wealth generating, industrialised economy. Prosecuting wars, occupations and annexations is not easy or cheap, but when talented inventors, flush with scientific advancements and financial resources, turned their sights toward the mechanisation of war, there were few Eastern armies able to resist. Professional, well-equipped and highly trained military forces took the Eastern world by storm.

Within a few generations, the British Empire had eclipsed the military accomplishments of Rome and outclassed the early Arab conquests. It had become the first contemporary superpower. This was all achieved through the widespread pursuit of economic freedom with minimal taxation and government interference. To give a striking example of the level of government activity in the British economy when the Empire reached its pinnacle, the tax rate in Britain during and preceding this point was a mere 10%. Compare that with the United Kingdom's current socialistic tax rates of over 40% and its now relatively humble position as a world power.

History is littered with the corpses of nations which sought to recreate paradise on earth through socialism. To follow this lead is folly; to ignore the lessons, is negligent. Although many deny it, free trade and free enterprise is miraculous in what it is capable of achieving. We have seen the value of trade, charity, enterprise and investment throughout the world. It is these that have provided sustained benefit to all segments of societies. They enable prosperity, eradicate poverty, create art, and provide leisure and comfort in the minds of the free.

No other system in human history has clothed so many, fed so many, and led so many to comfort, dignity and independence. No other phenomena or government has ever uplifted so many men, women and children from the soul-destroying ravages of poverty, material degradation and want. But free trade, charity and enterprise are not the inventions of mere mortals, they are Qur'anic exhortations and commandments, and they constitute the beautiful Sunnah of the Noble Prophet (peace be upon him). They are a divine blessing that we fail to appreciate and often even acknowledge.

Over the decades, misguided political leaders have led Pakistan in the direction of the Western model, but they imposed the contemporary socialist model instead of the enlightened and proven free market laissez-faire model of our Islamic yesteryear. They attempted to mould the primitive and fragile economy of Pakistan along the lines of the advanced Western economies. They foolishly confused the notion of '*modernisation*' with '*westernisation*'. These things are not the same.

True enough, there are many aspects of Western culture that are worthy of emulation: the rule of law, tolerance, fairness and honesty, but similarly there are many more aspects that are not. Aspiring to modernity does not mean copying Western culture wholesale, with all its decadence and immorality. We can keep our superior culture but still acquire the advanced technology and methods that will help us pursue our goals. Westernisation is not the answer; the path to prosperity for the masses lies in a system which leads to modernisation on our own terms.

But all socialism has given us is the moral corruption of Western culture without the essential modernisation that we needed. For all these years we have been on a fool's errand. Our leaders brazenly aped futile policies: nationalisation, high tariffs on foreign trade, labour laws, price controls, industrial and agricultural subsidies, anti-business regulation, public works, population control measures and more. Yet modernity seems further out of reach than it ever was, and worse still, our society is now riddled with Western depravity. We have succeeded in morally, spiritually and economically crippling our society in the same way the West is now fading. But what is a quiet, decadent decline for Western nations is, in many ways, life-threatening for Pakistan. Pakistan simply can't afford it.

No one can have failed to notice the despondency, helplessness and desperation in the air. We have been floating aimlessly for far too long. But it is not yet too late. The American author Henry David Thoreau once wrote, *"Not until we are lost do we begin to understand ourselves."* Well, our time for reflection and understanding has surely come. We can do better than this. We have much to be proud of: a great history, culture, and fine traditions and customs that appeal to the very best of man's spirit. The very principles of our Islamic outlook inspire honesty, frugality, honour, hospitality, diligence and hard work.

It is time to shed the pitiful Western complex that has plagued us for so many a long year. We must do this if we wish to look forward to a future of confidence and independence, a future where our nation is a beacon of light and inspiration to the entire world. If we strive for change, I know that one day soon, Pakistan will be admired and revered across the world when she fulfils the manifest destiny that our forefathers envisioned for her, and that the Ummah desperately requires of her.

In the beautiful words of Madr-e-Millat Fatima Jinnah, *"The immediate task before you is to face the problem and bring the country back on the right path with the bugles of Quaid-e-Azam's message. March forward under the banner of star and crescent with unity in your ranks, faith in your mission and discipline. Fulfil your mission and a great sublime future awaits your enthusiasm and action. Remember: 'cowards die many times before death; the valiant never taste death but once.' This is the only course of action which suits any self-respecting people and certainly the Muslim Nation."*

How can this be done? It is the subject of the following discussion.

1

ON LIBERTY

"Nobody can give you freedom. Nobody can give you equality
or justice or anything. If you're a man, you take it."

Malcolm X

A millennia and a half ago, the known world was dark and foreboding. The Arabs of the Arabian Peninsula were backward and disunited, ignored by the rest of the world. To their East, the tyrannical Sassanid Persians held sway over a vast territory with a highly centralised government and a rigid caste system. Religious and economic persecution was routine. To the West, the Roman Empire had collapsed and a successor empire, Byzantium had emerged from the fray. Like Rome before it, it was renowned for its imperial decadence, oppressive taxes, duplicitous politics and complex bureaucracy. Europe was in the worst shape of all, with warring tribes and barbarians; Goths, Huns, Vandals, Visigoths and more, dominating the continent. These truly were the Dark Ages.

The two great powers tussled with each other for dominance and dominion and few paid heed to the poor and backward tribes of the sun-blasted Arabian Peninsula. Although they were geographically in the midst of the known world, the vast and hostile desert sands provided a powerful natural cover from invasion and interference. Not that it mattered; nothing of consequence was thought to reside in Arabia. What little contact the world had with the Arabian peoples came in the form of the intermittent trading caravans that occasionally braved the desert sands. Travellers to the region noted that the only things that concerned these motley tribes were their barbaric traditions, water sources, ferocious blood feuds, fondness for poetry and their diligent worship of pagan idols.

What happened next is one of the most incredible tales in human history, and all based around an idea; the idea of liberation, sweeping away the old barbarism and ushering in a new age. It is said that all of the armies of the world cannot hold back an idea whose time has come; it is certainly true in this case. The Islamic faith changed the world forever, and within just a few years of its meteoric arrival, all the tribes and factions of Arabia were united behind a simple and powerful message. Energised by a dynamic creed and total faith in Allah, they swept out of the peninsula and within a hundred years or so had defeated the two warring superpowers of Persia and Byzantium and conquered most of the known world, from Spain and North Africa, to Persia, India and beyond.

This astonishing breakthrough started with a young orphan boy named Muhammad (peace be upon him) borne to the prominent Banu Hashim clan. Illiterate and under the protection of his aristocratic wider family in the trading town of Mecca, he grew up to pursue a remarkable talent for business and trade. He was highly intelligent, exquisitely handsome, humble, charismatic, and scrupulously honest. His noble character and his perfect conduct with everyone who met and knew him meant that he was widely admired, respected and trusted. So much so, that he was often asked to arbitrate during bitter disputes between rival tribes. His reputation only grew, and he became known as 'Al-Amin' (The Trustworthy).

Through his growing repute for natural honesty and his inclination for fairness in his business dealings, he came to the attention of a wealthy widow by the name of Khadija (may Allah be pleased with her). She asked him to partner with her in her flourishing business. He consented, and in time, the sheer perfection of his character, manners and conduct impressed her so much that she proposed marriage. They prospered together and lived a happy life for many years, but Muhammad (peace be upon him) was often troubled and disillusioned by the confusing and contradictory society around him. Always shunning the worship of idols, and the barbaric, immoral religious and cultural practices of the time, he preferred time alone and often retreated to the mountains near Mecca for quiet contemplation and meditation.

Then came the moment that would change the world. On one of these excursions he witnessed the presence of the Archangel Gabriel, who commanded him *"Read."* Shaken, he replied that he could not. The Archangel commanded him *"Read,"* twice more, becoming more emphatic each time. Distressed and in shock, Muhammad (peace be upon him) withdrew and rushed home to his beloved wife who believed his narration and consoled him. She became the first person to embrace Islam.

That night, he had commenced his Prophethood and experienced the first of many divine revelations that would form the entirety of The Holy Qur'an. Drawing strength and inspiration from the Almighty, in time he ventured out into Meccan society and preached the message of peace, monotheism and truth. His words were completely revolutionary, contradicting the traditional rites and bloodthirsty practices of the time.

His message to them: there is only one God, Allah, the God of your father Abraham, the God of Noah, Joseph, Moses and Jesus (peace be upon them all); Men should live in brotherhood and peace; No man is superior to any other except in his piety; Racism and arrogance is sinful; The giving of charity to the poor is an obligation of the wealthy; Men and women are equal in their rights to life, liberty and property; All should honour and be kind to their parents; The property of one is a sacred trust to all others; All trade and business should be conducted honestly. Further, all men are free by birth: Man is God's trustee on Earth; Men and women are at liberty to conduct their affairs with free will and all are responsible for their spiritual destinies.

Underpinning the notion of freedom was the notion that no mere mortal could intercede between God and the believers: no priest, idol, bureaucrat, or worldly noble or king. Little wonder then that in the midst of the oppression and stagnation of its neighbours, the Islam of Arabia was a beacon of light and hope. Little by little, the idea of personal, spiritual and economic liberty took hold and spread. By the time the Prophet (peace be upon him) passed away in 632 AD, all of the errant tribes of Arabia had been unified under the Islamic banner.

Then came the era of the Khilafat-e-Rashidun, or the Rightly Guided Caliphs. These great men oversaw the continuation of the most utopian society in world history. This did not go unnoticed. Satanic forces conspired beyond Muslim lands and the Muslim conquests of Persia and Byzantium followed as major battles ensued on both the western and eastern fronts. The Battle of Yarmūk, fought near Damascus in 636 AD, saw a small Muslim army defeat a much larger Byzantine force, permanently ending Byzantine rule south of Asia Minor. In the same year, a Muslim army achieved victory over a larger Persian force in the Battle of al-Qādisiyyah, near the banks of the River Euphrates (modern Iraq). During the course of the battle, the Sassanid army was routed.

Within a few decades, all the lands from Spain in the West to India in the East were absorbed into the Islamic World. Powerful ideas quickly overran prevailing customs and integrated into local cultures. Hundreds of thousands flocked to the faith, and with newfound economic liberty and an end to injustice and repressive taxation, a new trading empire was born. As the years passed, Muslim traders flourished and travelled beyond the lands of Islam, from Scandinavia to modern-day Indonesia, spreading the word of God through their example as they did so.

Did Islam conquer, or did it liberate? People speak often of the former, but it was surely liberation. Before Islam, the Byzantine Empire had grown increasingly despotic and intolerant, becoming brutally oppressive in its attitude to any religion or faith apart from Orthodox Christianity. At first the Orthodox Christians bickered amongst themselves over the nature of the faith and over controversies such as the Trinity. Then they actively persecuted those who did not share their beliefs, including Jews, Nestorians, Jacobites, Copts and pagans.

By around 600 AD, 'heretics' were under enormous pressure as they were increasingly brutalised by the Byzantine authorities. By then most who sought independent thought had escaped to Persia, which was only a little less tyrannical. Worst still, not only did the constant Byzantine-Persian wars devastate the inhabitants of these lands, but they only deepened the conditions of constant fear.

This then is the background to the rapid rise and tremendous success of early Islam. Islam stood for peace, social harmony, voluntary exchange and an end to tyranny. The conversion of non-Muslims to Islam was no priority for the Caliphate. After all, taxation was collected in the form of a head tax, and non-Muslims had to pay a slightly higher rate than Muslims. Thus non-Muslims under the Caliphate tended to bring in more revenue. Even still, other than the nominal 'Jizya' tax, which was very slight in comparison with the punitive Byzantine and Persian tax regimes, non-Muslims were treated as equal citizens, and left alone to live and worship as they wished.

Muslims lived alongside Hindus, Jews, Christians and others in harmony. But as Islam spread, its message found eager and willing converts. Muslims were truly free. In total contrast to earlier times, women could actually claim their rights and could thus own and inherit property. The State had a minimal role in economic affairs. Crucially, the unalienable rights of people were enforced through a rigid and wisely enforced law system called the Shariah, and primitive tribal, cultural and racial prejudices were abandoned.

When seen in this light, the success of the spread of Islam and its continuing hold on the hearts and minds of hundreds of millions cannot have been achieved through violent intimidation and forced conversions at the point of scimitars, but through the powerful message of peace, personal liberty and of course, divine providence. Islam is not tyrannical in nature, and thus needed no tyrannical methods for its expansion.

The people enduring life under the draconian superpowers of Persia and Byzantium with their rigid and oppressive systems were not conquered, but liberated. In the end, this newly acquired virtual freedom of thought spawned great progress in science, mathematics, astronomy, economics, art, culture, philosophy, poetry and architecture. The first great universities were established, and there was a complete absence of formality or oppressive State restrictions. The great Greek works were translated and examined, finally being taken seriously after a thousand years of neglect.

Most Muslims today are aware of the so-called Islamic Golden Age, but only in superficial terms. They never hear of the economic system that first established and fuelled it. Let us bear in mind that in the early years of Islam, in contrast to the deviances that we witness today, the basic principles of the economic aspects of the faith were followed to the letter and spirit. This set the foundation for trade, prosperity and progress and ignited the industry of the faithful. It was only much later that these sound principles were abandoned.

The early Caliphs understood that productivity and wealth were bestowed by the will of Allah. They knew that by following the clear precepts set out in the Holy Qur'an regarding property rights, honest trade and fair measures, this would be enough to ensure the prosperity and harmony of society. They saw it as inevitable - a divine blessing from the Almighty that would naturally result from simply following divine commandments. They were right. What we recognize today as Adam Smith's 'invisible hand' that guides the 'general interest' through personal self-interested activity, they saw simply as the natural and divine allocation of the bounty of the Creator amongst his creation. Just one more blessing amongst countless others.

The Shariah demands the protection and enforcement of property rights and ownership of land and assets, regardless of gender, ethnicity, religion, or social background. Muslim and non-Muslim men and women had rights granted by the Shariah which allowed them to buy, sell, mortgage and inherit land for farming, trade or any other purpose. All women were granted full and total rights to their property for the first time in history. This had sparked a great deal of resistance from the early pagan clan chiefs and elders who were more used to treating women like livestock. But the divine law was supreme, and violations were punished. Every major financial or social transaction was enforced through contracts and arbitrators. Whether for a loan, commerce, employment or even marriage, Islam stipulated that contracts had to be signed and copies kept by both parties.

The provision of property rights, liberty and the rule of law were critical in promoting the economic and cultural development of society. Agricultural advancements lead to increased subsistence and a higher level of economic security. Poverty in what was once a desolately poor society was markedly reduced as the new dynamic economic system advocated greater charity and private generosity. This ensured wealth for all citizens, and a higher quality of life than people had ever seen. Donors wishing to distribute alms even struggled to find recipients in need and willing to take them.

Increased trade brought increased choice, and countless trading caravans brought exotic plants and vegetables from far-flung lands. Orchards of citrus fruit and olives became a common sight, with souks, market gardens and parks springing up in every Muslim city. This was all underpinned by a sound and honest monetary system based on the expanding levels of circulation of a stable gold and silver coinage called the dinar and dirham. It brought stability and prosperity to the furthest reaches of the Islamic world through the integration of multiple monetary regions that had previously been separate and independent.

Apart from safeguarding the coinage, collecting taxes, upholding the law and court system, distributing the charity tax, and organizing and dispatching the army, the Islamic government had little else to do. It was not involved in the minutiae of economic life, and nor could it find reasons to be in the Holy Qur'an and Prophetic traditions. As long as something wasn't expressly forbidden by divine law, it was permitted.

Nowadays leaders trumpet 'Islamic-socialism', calling people to hark back to the Golden Age of the 'Islamic welfare state'. But they are misinformed. The Golden Age of Islam was underpinned not by anything akin to modern welfare socialism but clearly by free markets and individual industry. When we look back at that age what we see is the rule of law, the protection of property rights, minimal government intervention, private ownership of resources, a sound currency, low taxation, and economic and political freedom - these are the hallmarks of *free enterprise*. Distribution of wealth occurred through the Zakat tax for the poor, orphans and widows, but it was hardly comparable to the prodigious welfare states and crude government interventions that are espoused by politicians today all over the Muslim world.

Social welfare during the early Caliphate was optimal and minimal in its size in comparison to the rest of the economy. The early rulers did not want to breed a sense of dependence and helplessness among the Muslims. They wanted to encourage a sense of self-confidence, self-reliance and independence. The State did not pretend that it could solve all of the people's problems. Islam recognizes not the State or the rulers, but Allah as the ultimate Provider and Nourisher. Allah is the true source of all bounty and blessings. It was well known that private charity, brotherhood, solidarity and generosity were what were best to help the poor and needy. The Holy Qur'an champions these ideals and commands not the State, but individual men and women to take care of their families and neighbours who need help.

Much to the grievous loss of Muslims all over the world today, the fact that the early Islamic Caliphate between the 7th - 12th centuries was based on the earliest forms of free enterprise has been completely ignored. Even leaders and parties across the Muslim world who see themselves as more Islamically inclined regularly denounce the market-driven system that so catalyzed the growth and progress of Islam in its early years. This ignorant worldview is a great loss to over a billion Muslims suffering under the economic tyranny of socialism - to be told by misinformed leaders that socialism represents the ultimate in divinely inspired social justice, when in fact, modern socialism would have been an anathema to the early Muslim leaders.

Competent Western historians who have studied the Golden Age have tried to describe the system best as *'merchant capitalism'*. Whatever you wish to call it, it certainly worked. Pre-industrial Europe copied this model from the highly successful Ottoman Caliphate and implemented it in their own lands, beginning in the Italian princely states. It later spawned Industrial Revolutions and brought power, wealth and colonies. It was only in the early 20th century that this model would mutate beyond all recognition into the *'modern inflationary capitalism'* that we all endure today. But this modern system with its pretence of justice underlined by immoral interest based credit markets and inflationist central banks would have been as much of an anathema to the early Muslims as Socialism or Communism.

According to the Holy Qur'an and the Sunnah, there is nothing wrong with free trade and commerce. God encourages mankind to travel the land and seas and seek His bounty. For much of his life, our Noble Prophet (peace be upon him) was a merchant by profession, and his honesty and diligence brought him success. Ironically, Muslim leaders today speak of free enterprise and free trade in damning terms while conveniently ignoring both our Prophet's (peace be upon him) own occupation and the fact that some of the first innovations in global business were introduced by pioneering merchants and traders during the peak of Islamic civilization. The epic caravan trails of the Silk Route and Spice Route and the countless historical souks and markets in every Muslim town and city from Calcutta to Timbuktu pay testimony to the truth.

It was in the early Islamic world that the earliest trading companies and organizations were established. These were organizations similar to modern multinational corporations and functioned independently from State authorities. They worked with contracts, bills of exchange, credit, exchange rates, hedging, and existed in the form of partnerships (mufawada) and capital investments (mudaraba). During the 11th - 13th centuries in what is now modern Turkey, the earliest multinational organizations were established and were known as the 'Karimis'. These were business groups owned and controlled by entrepreneurs and came to play a great role in international trade in the Islamic world economy.

Islamic free enterprise worked because of its emphasis on justice, charity and fairness. It was promoted and developed according to the highest ethical values. The prohibition of usury in the Holy Qur'an in no way impeded the development of capital in any way. In fact, with the sound monetary system, it was a far more honest, fair and stable climate for business and employment. During the Golden Age and particularly between the 9th and 12th centuries, 'free enterprising' merchants were at the height of their success, and the Muslim economy flourished to the benefit of all. People of all faiths migrated from far flung lands to settle in Baghdad, Damascus, and Grenada. After all, the Muslim world was free, and it was the place to be.

* * * * *

Muslim power began to decline for many reasons. Apart from the deviations from the true practice of the faith, divisions between Sunnis and Shiites, among other groups, caused the followers of the Prophet (peace be upon him) to splinter and turn on each other. Many local rulers decide to set themselves up as virtual despots. In time, more and more resources and production began to be appropriated and monopolized by the State.

Not much different to today, as the Caliphate grew more self-absorbed and extravagant, the grand palaces accumulated courtiers and parasites who flattered the rulers in return for massive estates, fortunes and other favours. The economy became less meritocratic and more corrupt. Those with connections and influence prospered, leaving the vast bulk of the people far behind. Inept hereditary rulers and the compromise of honest practices and the rule of law caused what was a vibrant economy to stagnate and wither. This extinguished any potential spark of industrialisation.

The creep of proto-socialism and kleptocracy played a significant role in the waning of Islamic power, but a major aspect was the increasing debasement of the dinar and the dirham - the primary monetary units of the Middle East and beyond. For hundreds of years, prosperity and stability had been built on the solid foundation of the gold and silver standard. As commanded by Qur'anic law with regards to the provision of *"fair weights and measures"*, for centuries rulers and sultans took great care to maintain the weight and purity of the coinage. Mints all over the Islamic world, including Spain, were churning out dinars with a weight of no less than 4.25 grams, a weight first established under the reign of the Rightly Guided Caliphs and inherited from the Old Roman gold standard.

The gold standard worked wonders for hundreds of years until a dangerous new discovery was made. As Muslim caravans traversed the world, many travellers went to China along the Silk Route. In China, the Yuan Dynasty had created a unified, national money system that was not backed by any commodity. They instituted the world first 'fiat' paper currency. Transactions involving gold or silver were prohibited and Chinese warlords printed money at will to satisfy their spending needs. Of course, this caused rampant inflation. Inevitably, their currencies regularly collapsed and had to be replaced with new ones. This exposure of Muslim traders to the new 'paper currency' system was to have far-reaching effects in the Islamic world.

Chinese printing presses were a very useful invention for the ruling sheikhs who needed to pay for their extravagant lifestyles, cronyism and wars. For the first time, rulers had no need of hard gold or silver to back the money supply. Thus the practice of 'fiat' paper money quickly grew. The result could not have been unexpected because it went counter to the sound advice of the Qur'an. It was ultimately disastrous. The ability for weak rulers to print money at will was simply too great a temptation for them to stay disciplined for long.

The resulting rabid inflation began to destroy economic confidence, trade and growth. The elites and their cronies became richer, and the poor and middle classes were ravaged by rising prices and a precipitous decrease in their standard of living. Islam suffered from many other problems at the time, but the conversion from the classic gold and silver standard to a non-commodity paper currency proved to be an intense catalyst in the destruction of Islamic world power.

As the monetary dominance of Islamic civilisation declined, the gold standard baton passed to Western Europe via the vigorous Italian princely states. There were still bursts of progress, but much of the Muslim world fell into a prolonged period of division, misery and despotism. To this day, we have not recovered. In the absence of the natural financial checks that the gold standard provided to prevent government excesses, the personal freedom and liberty of individuals were dashed. Eventually, the Muslim nations and tragically, the Caliphate itself, became prey to the Western powers.

During the dark ages of Europe, it was the prosperity and vitality of the Islamic World that kept the ideals of civilization and honest money alive. In a dark world, Islam was a ray of light. It still is, but much diminished because of the ineptitude of continuous rulers who deviated from the straight path. But let we forget, the Islamic monetary system that is now only a footnote in history was crucial in Islam's success. The gold dinar was a *currency par excellénce*. Used as the standard medium of exchange all over the world, dinars are often still dug up in Africa, India, Scandinavia and even England. Of course, unlike the inflationary paper currencies of the time, the coins are still 'worth their weight in gold'.

Unlike the modern misguided socialistic interpretations of Islamic economics today, the economy of the Golden Age flourished because it operated around the idea of personal and economic liberty under Shariah law. The classical Islamic state did not interfere where it had no jurisdiction or permission as granted by the Qur'an and Sunnah. The early free enterprise that resulted from the accurate application of the law regarding economic matters was highly successful, hence the breathtaking spiritual, material, and scientific achievements of that era.

The Caliphate aimed to create a sphere in which individuals were free to think, choose and act within the confines of the Shariah without being restrained by an overbearing and domineering government. There were no grandiose visions of what could be achieved by the State. God was seen as the Supreme Judge and Provider and the State simply a vehicle to protect the Muslim citizenry by enforcing the divine law and living by it too. Government authority was never an instrument of tyranny, oppression and mass control as it has now become in so many Muslim nations.

The achievements of the free enterprise framework that underpinned the finest hour in Islamic history speak for themselves and as such, 'Islamic free enterprise' needs no propagandists. Today, as we grasp aimlessly in the darkness for a way out of our predicament, the greatest defence we have against poverty and tyranny is actually part of our glorious heritage. We need only revive an Islamic framework that maximizes the awesome potential for human growth and progress. History has proven beyond doubt that it is the efficacy of Islamic free enterprise that makes possible a stable, prosperous and contented society with a continually improving standard of living.

When elitism is such a burden on our backs, why do we not return to our Islamic roots when great men and women walked the land and great deeds were accomplished for the glory of Islam? We know it is possible, because we did it once before. Our forefathers lived in a land where all were on a level playing field and the State could not dispense unfair favours for some at the expense of all others. Exceptionally gifted individuals were at liberty to prosper and turn the proceeds of the fruit of their labour to others less fortunate - all in a voluntary fashion. Yet today many scoff and consider these ideas an anachronism of a bygone era. Why then can they not present us with a better system? Socialism? Capitalism? Communism? Fascism? All have failed.

While only socialistic conditions prevail in the much greater part of the Muslim world today, freedom and prosperity are accessible only to an elite minority of people. True 'Islamic free enterprise' provides the conditions by which every person is furnished with a favourable chance of striving after what is in the best interests of themselves, their families and their communities. It is these conditions which combined in the Golden Age to achieve an environment of confidence, opportunity and stability. All citizens were uplifted and empowered to work hard and persevere in freely fulfilling their obligations to their Creator and for their own personal growth and edification.

Commonly heard reproaches against free enterprise often level the charge that it facilitates a crude and ugly materialism that degrades moral and spiritual growth and culture. Yet that would assume that a government dominated society could achieve a superior culture through its own rough interventions and through the force of coercion. Do we see such a society today? The practical reality of the world today clearly illustrates that it is socialism that degrades morals and spiritual values by replacing absolute trust in God with a false and misplaced trust in the State. Just take a look around you. A socialistic system creates despair, poverty and stagnation. Of course it does. No truly moral system could ever be built by a deliberate organization of production through our illogical man-made regulations.

2

ON PROPERTY

"When neither their property nor their honour is
touched, the majority of men live content."

Niccolo Machiavelli

H uman rights are often discussed and debated in polite
circles. The media is infatuated with them and protestors
faithfully march for them. But there exists a profound
misunderstanding about the very nature of these rights. Many
opinions can be heard on the matter of what constitutes a right
and what does not, it is true however, that the fundamental
rights of human beings are sacrosanct. Fourteen centuries ago
Islamic law elaborated on a practical code of universal human
rights that was applicable to all: men, women, rich, poor, Arab
and non-Arab alike.

Rather than mere rhetorical flourishes and utopian notions,
these were practical and germane rights which aim at
conferring honour and dignity on mankind and eliminating
exploitation, oppression and injustice. Human rights in Islam
are firmly rooted in the belief that God, and God alone, is The
Cherisher and the source of all human rights. Due to their
divine origin, no leader, State, assembly or authority can

restrict or violate them. These rights are inherent, and cannot be surrendered or abrogated.

These divinely-gifted rights to life, liberty and property must all be maintained and upheld in any economic system that is instated by man. Fundamentally, human life is considered sacred in the eyes of God. The Holy Qur'an mentions how the killing of one person is considered equivalent to the killing of the whole of mankind. In many other places, the Holy Qur'an emphasizes how mankind and jinn are unique amongst creation because they are born free and endowed with free choice and rational faculties (at their own peril). Thus they are just as free to be 'the lowest of the low' as they are to attain the highest character and station. The Muslim faith spread rapidly precisely because it exemplified this powerful message of liberty to those who had suffered under imperialism and tribalism. People flocked to Islam because it swept away corrupt and tyrannical customs. Freedom from tyranny and slavery was popular, and it still is.

But human rights can tend to be somewhat nebulous concepts. How are they enforced or expressed? The answer lies in the fact that a *right* relates to a person as a property owner. When we assert that we have a 'right to life', the implication is that we are the *custodian* of our lives. This does not mean that we have complete control and can choose to stay happy, healthy or alive forever; it means that no one can 'take' our lives from us unless it is for lawful reasons (for instance, if we have committed a capital crime).

Our lives are a sacred trust gifted by God which we own and are responsible for - our lives are our property, and nobody can arbitrarily violate us through coercion, violence or intimidation. We have a *right* to be free because we own ourselves and are endowed with free choice and will be held individually accountable for what we do: good or evil. These rights are noble in themselves, but they only have real value when they are universally applicable and do not apply to simply a chosen few. Also, being God-gifted, a 'human right to liberty' is a kind of intrinsic property which cannot be sold or transferred. Tangible and even intangible property can be sold and transferred from one person or organisation to another, but individuals cannot auction away their rights.

In pre-Islamic Arabia, and only until recently in the West; women had no real rights: they did not own themselves and could not own property. Women were considered the property of their husbands, fathers or guardians: they could not sign contracts on their own behalf and thus had no freedom. In legal and cultural terms most women were considered subhuman, chattels and equivalent to slaves. The guidance of the Noble Prophet (peace be upon him) brought revolutionary changes to society because henceforth women were able to legally own, inherit and dispose of property freely. Importantly, women could sign contracts without threat or coercion whether for marriage, commerce or anything else. For the first time ever, they could *all* do so on an equal basis with men. Islam swept away chauvinism and oppression in its wake fourteen centuries ago. It was only as recent as the 20th century that the Western world caught up.

The Noble Prophet (peace be upon him) stated in his final sermon that his followers were to *"regard the life and property of every Muslim as a sacred trust,"* and that *"nothing shall be legitimate to a Muslim which belongs to a fellow Muslim unless it was given freely and willingly."* This clearly indicates the enormous importance of the role of private property in a Muslim society. Thus any person has the right to seek to own anything lawful as long as he accepts that all those he deals with posses identical rights. A person has sovereign control over his property and can do with it as he wishes, but only if it is *honestly* acquired and utilised. His behaviour must not affect others adversely or infringe on their rights. The revelation of Allah is clear: *"O you who believe! Do not appropriate each other's property and wealth in a manner that is unjust: Rather, let trade be transacted in a manner that brings mutual satisfaction..." (The Holy Qur'an, 4:29).*

Violating another person's property is equivalent to violating the right to 'acquire and own property', and thus, is a violation of their fundamental human rights. This is a serious crime. To reflect this, Shariah punishments tend to be relatively harsh in order to strongly deter criminality and ensure stability and peace. The punishment for repeated theft (a property violation), is the amputation of a hand. This may seem draconian to the sensibilities of the modern world, but it is merely a reflection of the sheer seriousness with which the Islamic world-view regards the rights of property ownership - the basis of all human rights. Property violations, whether they arrive in the form of theft, damage or trespass, are considered high ranking crimes that must be deterred through the prospect of harsh punishment. The old legal adage *'the punishment must fit the crime'* is apt here.

Let us be clear. Rights are not granted by leaders, constitutions or legal ordinances. They are inherent in the make-up of man. Governments and legal documents are necessary to safeguard the violation of intrinsic rights but they do not grant them. Crucially, the creation of divisions within society such as an elite class cannot be countenanced because no man should be able to acquire rights in such a way as to lessen or diminish the rights of another. And in practical terms, the most basic right of freedom of will and action is underpinned by the right of a free person to own *property* and be the master of it.

Property violations cause havoc in society in numerous ways. They are emblematic of certain people's misguided opinions that they are superior to others and thus hold an *a priori* right to steal, destroy or trespass over anything or anyone they please. Such an ethos can only lead to moral and social disorder. The problem with our society is that an elite few violate other people's lives and properties with little or no impediment. Here, rights are not equal for all: those in positions of power are *special* as they possess 'extra' rights at the expense of all others. However, *true* justice is blind: either all people must have equal rights or no concept of human rights is possible at all. If some people can violate the property of others even through 'legal' means then we require a change in terminology. We would have to say that acquiring, owning and safeguarding property in this case is not a right, but is in fact a *privilege* that is knowingly or unknowingly bestowed by the authorities.

If someone's *privileges* are withdrawn at the whim of the State and his property is violated in some way, he will have no ability to protect it and will find no real protection in the law. Thus he will be prevented from defending his fundamental God-given rights in comparison to the violator. It will only take a moment of reflection for us to realize that we live in a society where the privileges of a tiny minority supersede the basic rights of all. It is an unacceptable state of affairs.

In Pakistan, many politicians and opinion leaders wax lyrical about notions of social justice. We know that the reality on the ground however, is very different. In practice, rights are mere temporary political privileges. Indeed, it is a lawless society where politicians, government beaurocrats, police and corporate elites comprise of a class of permanently privileged people - beyond the reach of justice and accountability. Their victims consist of the rest of society - a class of people whose rights may or may not be upheld depending on the whim of the State. This is the famous 'egalitarianism' of socialism in practice.

In our country, the notion of equal rights for all men as property owners has never been appropriately recognized: no person's property is truly their own, nor is it ever truly safe from intrusion and violation from the privileged classes and the State. The consequences of this are highly damaging. A successful and stable economic system is reliant on the protection of property rights and the quick and just resolution of disputes regarding property and criminality. In an atmosphere where property owners are constantly denied their rights, what results is perpetual uncertainty and instability. Social order breaks down as individuals cannot operate confidently in the system.

The State and some classes of people are privileged in excess of what they deserve, and the manner in which they abuse their privileges is wrong. But this does not mean that privilege is wholly undesirable. When privileges are extended to a government through a consensual process and when steps are taken to restrain the privileged so that they do not violate the rights of others by binding them with a strong, independent legal system, they are not a bad thing. In fact, governments only function because the people bestow them with privileges to enact policies and govern on their behalf. But privileges must never supersede the inherent rights of others. This means that the property rights of all members of society should be protected at all times and against all threats - even from the government itself.

Unfortunately in Pakistan, the notion of private property rights is not practiced as it should be. The corrupting nature of command and control economics has done vast damage to the lives, liberty and properties of most of the 'under privileged'. Meanwhile, those in positions of power have benefited enormously. Due to our weak, substandard Western laws, the State has 'legally' assumed control of increasing portions of the national economy and the factors of production and in the process has trampled on the private property rights of the people. Such collectivizing measures lead to a situation where people do not have sovereign ownership of their own property. The assumption is that the State has a vested interest and right to interfere in everyone's lives, and that even the most banal activities must be conducted with authorization and permission from State beaurocrats.

This notion of socialistic collectivism leads to heavy handed regulations and restrictions on economic freedom. Useful and productive activity is hindered and sabotaged. When this happens, prosperity is undermined, economic growth is curtailed and poverty becomes all the more difficult to alleviate - all because markets are not free and people do not have sovereign rights to their property, labour and capital. This results in a throwback to the times of tyranny and barbarity which Islam swept away in the first instance. Nations and empires then were tyrannical because people were denied rights, taxes were punitive and only an elite few had the privileges of State protection. During that era, the State was primarily an agency for the 'legalised' and systematic expropriation of innocent people's property.

We have sleepwalked into this disorder. A State dominated economy is un-Islamic and immoral because it places some in positions of privilege and diminishes the rights of all the rest who are not in a similar position of power. It entrenches a sense of elitism and creates a multi-tiered society where some are subject to law and others are able to avoid the consequences of their misdemeanours through the vagaries and loopholes which they themselves create. With elite politicians, bankers and beaurocrats systematically chipping away at the people's rights to freedom and opportunity, social justice and prosperity are lethally compromised. People's property is not recognized or respected, and the result is poverty and despair. It is shameful then, that in spite of having the blessed light of Islam in our lives, we seem to have regressed back to the days of ignorance.

* * * * *

Under a socialistic system, many aspects of economic life are collectivized or under 'public ownership'. The problem with this is that it is inherently inefficient. When large swathes of land, labour and capital are owned and managed by the State, no private perspective can be maintained. When everyone owns something, rarely is anyone willing to take responsibility for it. For example, the air around us is gratis. It costs nothing to anyone and is effectively owned by the public who are thus at liberty to use it in any manner they choose. This means that many feel that they are free to pollute it with impunity while at the same time no-one has a vested interest in protecting it.

The State has no incentive to do it either, as it is a primary polluter and violator itself. The inevitable result can be seen and smelt in the choking fumes and pungent odours that infest our streets and towns. The same principle also applies with other public property such as parks, natural reserves, buildings and roads. There is little or no incentive for proper maintenance or innovation on sound management practices.

Only private ownership with sovereign control can enable true innovations and long term developments to take place which are in the interests of the property itself. What's more, only when this right is universally applied can such innovation not infringe on the rights of neighbours and the rest of society. The control of the owner is important, but it must stop at the edge of their property, and they are responsible and accountable for any damage they cause beyond the boundaries of their property if property rights are to be properly and correctly enforced.

Only through universally available private ownership of property can the dignity and productivity of people be maintained and upheld. If we want to further the development of a thriving and dynamic economy, we must look to privatise certain non-essential State functions. The State has no business owning parks, nature reserves or public buildings and the like. The State simply cannot maintain them in the true public interest.

It is a fact. Most property under public ownership deteriorates and degrades over time. It is inevitable. Note the awe-inspiring architectural monuments dotted around Pakistan. These phenomenal sites declare the glory and grandeur of Muslim civilisation at its height. They are an important part of our country's remarkable history and outstanding heritage, and yet under State ownership, held in 'the public interest', they are crumbling and being destroyed due to a lack of proper maintenance, attention and respect.

Private owners would never allow such a thing to happen. They would have the proper incentive to protect, maintain and invest in their property and open it to the public whether for profit or not. And yet when we ask who is responsible for the degradation of these historic and cultural sites, no answers are to be found. No one can be held to account because it is in the nature of beaurocrats to swiftly pass the buck of responsibility. But the blame does not lie with them. It is the system that is truly at fault - a system where authority is dispersed among faceless paper-pushers who have little or no incentive to go above and beyond the call of duty.

There is a very good reason why private property was designated *"a sacred trust"* by our Noble Prophet (peace be upon him). Private property allows resources to be utilised to their highest advantage, regardless of who owns them. What counts is the incentive that propels owners to do this. Governments do not have this incentive, and people tend not to respect and take care of property that is publicly owned. But privately owned property is another matter entirely. It does not matter who owns the property, even if it remains in a family line or a business, as long as it was honestly acquired and the law and people's freedom and rights are respected. The entire economy benefits regardless of who the owner is, wealthy or poor, advantaged or not.

In reality, as long as rights to property and freedom are equal for all and they are upheld in an even handed manner, economic growth and prosperity for all is generated. Even if property is not being utilised effectively under a private arrangement this does not last forever. Market forces soon push owners to act in order to maximise the value of their property by changing its use or transferring its ownership. Beaurocrats are insensitive to market forces, and so bad decisions tend to stick for a long time. In the market though, the price mechanism propels and enforces positive and efficient practices and soon corrects bad ones.

Property in private hands increases efficiency and productivity. With proper property rights and freedom, we can all be creative and generate goods, services and wealth that will enrich all society. Selling, sharing and giving are meaningless unless we are the owners of what is sold or given freely. If we own nothing, then we cannot contribute anything. Voluntary charity is to be encouraged, but a person can only give something away whether in charity or hospitality if he has a surplus from which to give, and if he has authority and responsibility in the ownership of what he is giving. Charity brings its own benefits - as long as it is voluntary and private. Unfortunately, politicians get this urge too, because they can bask in the warm glow of giving help conspicuously. The problem is that they do not give away what is theirs, but what is everyone else's, and thus they are often careless, self-serving and indeed, reckless about how they do it.

To maximize human well-being and to minimize disputes, private ownership and management of land should be implemented as much as possible. As long as the ownership is legal, an owner should have his property rights upheld and enforced efficiently and justly in the courts. Pakistan cannot progress, whether on its farms, in its industries, in its shops, or in its homes without the existence of true free markets, sound money, stability, and law and order assisted by universally recognised and enforceable property rights. This will propel economic growth and widen and deepen the level of prosperity in the nation. The ingredients are all known - they just need to be brought together by a responsible and sensible government that knows its place in the grand vision.

3

ON INCENTIVES

"My reading of history convinces me that most bad
government results from too much government."

Thomas Jefferson

Since the 19th century, some critics of the ever-growing State have called themselves 'individualists', an inaccuracy which ignores the obvious truth that many forms of useful human activity are not performed by individuals acting in isolation, but often by people in groups. The volunteers that flock to the scenes of natural disasters, and the charitable institutions that selflessly serve millions across our land, pay testimony to this fact. Such generosity and concern for others at one's own expense allows us to refute the dogmatic individualism that is borne of Margaret Thatcher's infamous quip, *"there is such a thing as society"*. In reality, the genuine concern of worth is not between individual and collective, but between the voluntary and the coercive.

Whether in the guise of families, companies, charities, political parties or even trade unions, collectives form the bedrock of human society and, provided they are formed on a voluntary and mutually agreeable basis and do not advance at the expense of innocents, they are beneficial. What is not voluntary however can only be coercive, and realistically only the State has the necessary considerable power at its disposal to literally 'command' obedience. It does so through the implied or overt threat of force. This force manifests itself in the form of taxes, fines, legislation, regulation and the potential criminalisation of the rebel. Thus, as a tool of socialist planners who wish to sculpt and chisel the world closer toward their utopian ideal, the irresistible machinery of the State is often used with impunity to plough roughshod over the individual and collective preferences of the masses.

In either its Leninist or more modest Fabian forms, socialism assumes that people cannot or will not deal with their lives by their own initiative and through cooperation unenforced and unregulated by the State. Seizing and deploying the apparatus of government gives planners a means to remedy the 'inevitable' failures of people acting by themselves in free enterprise. But no matter how hard they try, or how finely detailed their plans be, they can only fail.

The explanation for this can be found in the inherent psychology of the human mind. Socialisms primary failing lies in the cavalier attitude this ideology holds towards behavioural incentives. What is an incentive? Webster's Dictionary defines the term as *"...that which moves or influences the mind, or operates on the passions; that which incites, or has a tendency to incite, to determination or action; that which prompts to good or ill..."* Incentives are thus the encouragements that motivate people to make certain decisions over others. By offering certain rewards or even punishments to a subject, we will inspire or induce particular courses of action.

Of course, the sole purpose of any government policy is to change behaviours and attitudes towards those purposes that the government feels best suit the common good. It should only be expected then that the primary consideration of policymaking would be informed by the behavioural incentives of people on the receiving end. In an ideal world, we could presume that politicians would take the confines and vagaries of human nature into account when formulating policy. But alas we do not live in an ideal world, but in the real one, one in which our politicians still place credence in a discredited nonsensical ideology.

The socialistic weltanschauung is unbelievable, unconscionable and most of all, unworkable. It is based on a number of axioms that defy all credibility - mainly because they disregard the human condition. The policies that are borne out of this philosophy are based on these faulty foundations and are thus inherently flawed. For example, socialism assumes that industrial societies are a 'battlefield' on which class warfare is constantly being waged. On the good team are the keen and always diligent workers while the villains are the greedy and exploitative 'capitalists'. The dogmatic belief is that owners will not give labour its fair share of the proceeds of its work and industry unless coerced to do so, and that wealth must be forcibly distributed in society according to people's 'needs' (as defined by the ruling beaurocrats, not the people themselves) rather than according to their effort and performance.

Unfortunately the worst schemes in history have tended to be those that have the greatest mass popular appeal. Socialism is no exception. No rational individual wants to work harder then he possibly has to, and so the concept of a benevolent government taking care of him from the 'cradle to the grave' is appealing - maybe even more so if he is relatively poor and disadvantaged. This in itself is a clear incentive to vote for a socialistic party.

But this paternalistic attitude towards entire populations does profound damage to the day to day incentives that people are guided by as regards to their behaviour. The distortion of people's incentives to naturally struggle and strive for their futures and that of their families results in economic malaise, social degradation and ruin. This is inevitable, because as a direct result of socialistic policies, hard work, endeavour and success is punished, and lethargy and failure is rewarded and spurred on.

Some policies, like the laws of the land that punish criminal behaviour, are clearly indispensable. These are laws that prevent undesirable criminal and uncivil behaviour. But for planners in the midst of fashioning a socialist utopian paradise, all human activity is fair game. Whether this activity (however banal), is desirable or undesirable, lies totally at their discretion. Therefore, planners will occupy their time by micromanaging the lives of individuals and the operations of businesses to an absurd degree, and making their lives a misery in the process. Notwithstanding the fact that people and businesses are perfectly capable of handling their own affairs with equanimity, planners do not trust citizens to behave in what they would deem to be the correct way.

This poses a myriad of problems because the implementation of any policy may result in adverse affects, and thus may counteract the beneficial impacts of that policy in other seemingly unrelated areas of the economy. It cannot be assumed that an entity as complex as an economy will act in a single predictable way. An economy consists of countless different chains and linkages that are all interconnected and interdependent. Politicians formulating new policies would do well to bear in mind Cicero's penetrating question: 'cui bono', meaning 'who benefits?' Every policy will inevitably have unforeseen consequences, and many will benefit who were not initially intended to.

That is not a bad result perhaps, but the corollary is a lot worse. When cranking certain policy levers, many, many more will be harmed who were not meant to be harmed. Any policy that is designed to influence one part of an economy will always have indirect effects on other parts and it should not surprise us to hear that these counter-effects are often likely to be harmful and disruptive. This is where the root cause of the failure of the planners lies. They assume that by subsidising, taxing, rewarding, punishing, hindering, and encouraging certain sectors, they can micromanage their way to utopia. But they cannot.

* * * * *

The father of modern economics, Adam Smith, famously stated that if every individual pursued his own interest, the result would always be the betterment of all his fellow men.

Individuals can never be self sufficient; we cannot make all of our own clothes, grow all of our own food or totally administer to our own illnesses. At one point or another we must invariably rely on the work of others. But it is the incentive of every agent in the economy to maximise their own welfare that allows this work to be done at all. Every individual and business in an economy acts in a kind of chaotic unison to produce the multitude of goods and services that allow others to carry out their day to day lives. This is not achieved though government diktat. Adam Smith likened this division of activity and its efficient results to an 'invisible hand' that acts in an undirected way to fulfil individual and community wants and needs.

This occurs in spite of the fact that most people do not have the direct intention to help others by producing goods and services that others need but could not produce themselves. Every individual and business in an economy, when carrying out their legitimate daily business, is working in the public good and acting on behalf of the welfare of others by fulfilling wants and needs, whether they know it or not. In addition, the resulting competition between goods and services stimulates better efficiencies and productivity which brings about lower prices and higher quality products. All combine to increase real living standards for the common man.

The greatest value of free market systems is their ability to somehow enable people and businesses to utilise their resources and talents in a way that maximises output. When businesses have to compete for customers, they have a strong financial incentive to provide the best products and services possible at the best possible value. While survival amidst competition is the most persuasive of incentives, businesses soon understand the importance of marketing, quality control and effective sales methods.

The businesses that succeed in catering best for their customers gain a greater market share and higher profitability than less effective competitors. These businesses become attractive to investors and expand in size, employing more staff and spreading wealth. In this way, providing they stay efficient, the most productive and innovative businesses earn profits and grow. The least productive ones fall by the wayside, creating space for newer, more dynamic entrants.

The clear incentives that free market competition provides are fundamental in maximising innovation and invention in an economy. If a free market is not allowed to function because of excessive regulation and government action, then these incentives become distorted. The participants in the economy no longer base their decisions on incentives that would otherwise maximise productivity. Under a socialistic system, when making decisions on how best to utilise their resources, businesses must also take into account spurious factors such as red tape, legislation and tax incentives. For example, they may not be able to expand and take on more staff as rigid labour laws might prevent them from letting future employees go.

Regulations and legislation thus make the pursuit of some otherwise legitimate commercial activities unachievable. Through the powerful tool of legislation, it is possible to criminalise some activities or, more likely, create insurmountable hurdles for businesses to overcome. Affected businesses will soon conclude these are mountains not worth climbing. The amount of form filling and palm greasing that would be required no longer makes the objective worthwhile. But inconvenient regulations are often only the thin end of the wedge. Because planners believe that the private sector is incapable of making its own decisions, their work is never done. Ronald Reagan was not an economist, but his economic logic was faultless when he declared, *"If you want more of something, subsidize it; if you want less of something, tax it."* Thus the deluge of laws and largesse emanating from State offices carries all before it.

For example, subsidies are seemingly all the rage these days. Politicians crow about their generosity with other people's money. 'Flagship' or prestige industries are often the primary beneficiaries. But just because a politician insists that the country should have, for example an 'indigenous automotive sector' does not mean that he is right. Subsidising such industries diverts scarce resources that could be more efficiently used elsewhere. Cars are a consumer-good like any other, they have no special status in an economy. Having a car industry brings no more benefits than having a toaster industry, yet we do not hear politicians boasting about their latest subsidies to toaster manufacturers. Quite simply, if we get over our own ego's, we will find that there is simply no need to manufacture cars if it is significantly cheaper to import them. Far wiser, far more economically expedient to consume fewer resources by importing cheaper cars, and instead utilise more resources in sectors where one has a comparative advantage.

Prestige industries are mostly incurably unprofitable and unproductive and should really be put out of their misery. By ridding the economy of debilitating, uncompetitive blind alleys, we can identify business sectors offering a higher chance of creating genuine wealth and employment. Nevertheless, governments will declare some industries as 'too big to fail', and then indulge in generous bailouts at taxpayer's expense when such industries (inexplicably) fall into financial difficulty. Keeping them solvent and functioning is either a result of nationalistic egotism or an excessively optimistic but fruitless hope that they may become profitable in the future.

Of course, it is rare to find any major business or industry anywhere in the world where this miraculous turnaround has actually happened. This is because subsidisation does nothing to improve the incentives of these organisations to become more streamlined and productive - it only makes them ever more dependent on State munificence. When the State is prepared to prop up a failing business, it may seem irrelevant to the managers of that business what they do. In economic parlance, this is known as 'moral hazard'. The resulting *"carry on regardless, the State will bail us out,"* attitude will not result in decisions being made that are based on sound business principles.

With excessive government intervention, the incentives for anyone to act in the most naturally efficient way simply no longer apply. On a micro level, planners will use the taxation system as a blunt instrument to achieve their aims for social egalitarianism. To take an example, in a socialistic State it is typical to find very high income tax rates in the top brackets for the highest earning individuals. Effectively, the more an individual earns, the greater the percentage value of tax they will be paying as compared to those earning less.

This is done in order to redistribute wealth in the name of fairness. But not only is it unfair for one man to be paying a higher 'percentage' rate then another, but it also damages the higher earners incentive to work harder and to the best of his ability. Instead of treating this individual fairly, socialists would seek to penalise him and distort his incentives. Inevitably he will find it difficult to reconcile working hard and earning more with the fact that most of his efforts go straight to the treasury. The net result is less economic activity and less wealth for the economy. *Cui bono* indeed.

The diktats of bureaucrats are by and large neither useful nor necessary. If the objective is securing the highest level of efficiency and productivity of the economy, then existing regulations, tax and subsidy regimes must be reviewed. If, when interrogated, they show signs of bias towards particular industries, sectors and *especially* particular corporations, they should either be abolished or amended. At worst all policies should be 'incentive neutral'.

In Pakistan, if every individual freely specialises in the profession in which he is the most optimally productive, and when every business is allowed the freedom to invest in projects that are the most optimally productive, productivity will increase, national income will increase, wages will increase. Under or close to a free market regime, every input and resource will have been freely allocated to near its most optimum and productive use through the incentivising power of competition. While the State must help those individuals who are *truly* deserving of assistance, society will only become truly equal with a level playing field for all individuals when no one is given an unfair preference over anyone else. This is true social justice.

4

ON EDUCATION

"A little learning is a dang'rous thing; Drink deep, or taste not the Pierian Spring: There shallow draughts intoxicate the brain, and drinking largely sobers us again."

Alexander Pope

M any claim that the lack of literacy and education in our society is the primary cause of Pakistan's lack of development. Not true. In fact, those responsible for the catastrophes we are enduring have qualifications that are unmatched. Some have attended the most prestigious Western institutions and have returned with their heads over-brimming with ideas. Education is not a problem in our country; a more appropriate term would be 'mis-education'. For our leaders, this is where the trouble lies. Plato once remarked, *"the direction in which education starts a man will determine his life."* He was talking about indoctrination, and indeed, socialist leaning educational institutions spawn fruit that doesn't fall far from the tree. When their students eventually go on to govern countries, write opinion columns or teach youngsters, they do so according to how they have been taught.

True enough, there is a great deal of illiteracy in our society. But is an illiterate old man in interior Sindh, or a naive village girl in the Frontier Province responsible for Pakistan's failures?

Not at all. The fault lies not with them or with the millions of others who share their circumstances, but squarely at the feet of our illustrious leaders who put their grand theories into practice once arriving in high office. The result is before our eyes. Of course, it is the habit of cowards and tyrants alike to lay blame for their failures on innocents. Thus our elites can scarcely conceal their contempt for the 'unwashed masses' on whose ignorant condition they place responsibility for all the nation's ills. This insidious 'blame the victim' culture deserves to be exposed.

The reality is this: our leaders were taught to be socialistic; they have governed as socialists; they have created socialistic institutions and they implemented a mass education system along socialistic lines through which they propagate yet more Western socialism. Thus many generations in our country have been denied the ideology and philosophy of our Founding Fathers in favour of spurious Western theories that do incalculable harm. Yet Allama Iqbal and Quaid-e-Azam worked tirelessly to throw off the yoke of colonialism. They shunned Western philosophies and ideologies in favour of a uniquely Islamic, Pakistan-centric worldview that rejected all Western *"ism's"*. It is a tragedy that their successors lacked the confidence to take these noble ideals to their logical conclusion and instead fell for a mirage.

Our leaders continue to fall hook, line and sinker for fallacious Western schemes: price-fixing, nationalisation, Keynesian profligacy, colonial era law, protectionism, fiat paper currency - these are just a few of the many items in the import ledger. They implement failing systems that prioritise political expediency and economic immorality at the expense of real Islamic enlightenment and illumination. The fact that their *"little learning is a dang'rous thing,"* has been proven beyond any doubt. Around 2,000 years ago the Roman Historian Tacitus wrote words to the effect: *"Britons are very good at being Roman. They like the baths, the forum and they think they are becoming Roman whereas in fact these devices enslave them to Rome."* Replace Britons with "Pakistanis", and Roman with "Western", and the inherent problem is explained.

Due to the failures of our State educational institutions, and attempts by so-called liberals to erase any sense of patriotism from the minds of our youth, many now have a complete lack of understanding of the nations underpinning 'Iqbalian' ideology and its spiritual destiny. Of course it is not universally true; many of our youth defy the system - somehow. But it is rare to come across those who have resisted the propagandisation of society and have retained truly liberated minds, unencumbered by West-worship.

Not many will disagree when I say that our nation's mass education system is a total betrayal of our children. It blunts their intelligence, narrows their perspectives and wreaks havoc with their future prospects. Instead of churning out self-confident, savvy youngsters with a firm grasp of realities, physical and spiritual, it seems we only graduate drones that have a limited outlook, all based on Western oriented solutions to any given problem.

The point is that if our 'mass education' programme could be described as an institution, it would be institutionally 'unfit for purpose'. School buildings are basic and crumbling, some without even rudimentary furniture, resources are few; textbooks and syllabi are outrageously outdated and teachers are unmotivated and undertrained. Bureaucratic forces have defeated the government's best intentions. The result is that our children's futures, and to some degree their lives, are impoverished because they are enduring a system that is so fundamentally deficient.

Without any thought, foresight or long term vision, precious funds are poured into the black hole of bureaucratic educational machinery, never to see the light of day again. The State propaganda machine twists, spins and misguides with irrelevant factoids - the number of schools allegedly built, the number of students allegedly enrolled, and exaggerated improvements in the literacy rate. Yet even those who vocally criticise the failed education system do not question the policies themselves. They only argue for the government to accelerate its efforts and chide it for not doing more. What is little understood is that it is the education policy that is wrong, and when failing policies are accelerated, they only fail faster.

Change is desperately needed, along with a good dose of common sense. Ever since Pakistan's creation, the political and bureaucratic trend has been a mindless effort to replicate the methods of more mature nations. This has been done in a haphazard manner. Our ministers are blinkered to the obvious truth that Western nations have certain capabilities based on their wealth and institutions that allow their success. As of yet, we do not have these capabilities. They fail to understand that the reason a mature country may have success with an education policy may also be the same reason why a less mature country may fall short when implementing an identical policy.

To take a simple example, a mature nation may have a tried and tested administrational capacity that can easily lend itself to setting up and maintaining thousands of schools. But a poor and developing nation may not. If it tries to enact an identical policy in copycat fashion but without an efficient and reasonably accountable and honest beaurocracy, it will inevitably flounder. If we brought some common sense back into play, we would soon realise that aping more mature nations will not work, because we are not comparing like with like. Yet this is something our 'highly educated' leaders have been unable to fathom.

But the rot goes far deeper. As if this reality were not bad enough, once again, beaurocratic corruption raises its sinister head. A significant number of schools don't even exist except in the imaginations of bureaucrats in provincial capitals. These so called 'ghost' schools are simply the result of a corrupt and wholly inadequate bureaucrat system. Not only unfit is the system for such a vital task, but it does not even have the ability to incorporate simple checks and balances to prevent wholesale abuses of the system. The administrative and technical capacity of the State simply isn't up to it, and we must acknowledge that it never will be. Even the most advanced economies struggle with the heavy burden of running thousands of schools in a centralised fashion. If they cannot do it effectively with all their capabilities and technology, then we should not be 'the fools that rush in where angels fear to tread.'

Educating our youth, the flower of our nation, is a noble and pure endeavour. But our system has descended into an exploitation racket resulting in scarce funds being used only to line the pockets of traitorous, corrupt officials. The approach has failed because the principal agents in this process: parents, school management, local and federal officials, teachers, and children have not had the correct incentives to do what we would perceive to be the right thing. Yet, the privileged few, well able to afford good private education for their children, have remained relatively unscathed due to the luxury of being able to avoid the failed government sector. Able to sidestep State schools, they have opted for private, competitive schools that have been an excellent springboard for future success.

While our elite classes race ahead, government schools are failing a large and increasingly disillusioned underclass. Looking at the catastrophic results, it should be increasingly obvious that the answer to the problem of poor quality schools does not lie with mindless government spending on building yet more substandard schools. This approach has been implemented *ad absurdum* for far too long. Few would agree with the proposition that literacy rates have improved much. This is simply not acceptable. What is needed is a new, dynamic and yes, radical approach.

* * * * *

It is not a Herculean task to sweep these Aegean stables clean. The solution relies on some very simple principles. Many millions of parents cannot afford for their children to attend good private schools and must reconcile themselves to government schools, but why not give them a *choice*? Why not make these private schools *accessible* to the poorest? And why not enforce a robust, modern *curriculum* that works in the interests of our nation's future rather than undermines it? Our problems can be fixed once we resolve just these three things:

choice, accessibility and *curricula*. An ideal reformed education system will tackle all three simultaneously.

Firstly, *choice* - a solution must be found whereby all parents are able to freely exercise their choice on where to send their child. They can no longer be compelled to send their children to failing State schools. Government must relinquish its monopoly over the schools that cater to our poorest. As we are aware, the best way to improve products and achieve lower prices is not through government efforts, but through free market competition and consumer choice. Thus we must accept that the free market must be allowed to operate to improve the quality of education for all children. We must no longer think of children as statistical numbers on government educational reports. They are consumers looking to select the best value and highest quality service from their schooling.

We cannot escape the reality that government schools have been starved of the dynamism of competition, and this is the primary reason why so many have become dreary places of last resort. Government schools are immune to the market because they are technically 'free' and do not need to attract students or provide a decent education to survive. By not taking in fees, they are not financially accountable to parents and so they need not be concerned about their poor standards. On the other hand, market competitive schools must offer the highest quality education at the lowest possible cost. They vigorously compete with each other in order to attract and enrol students. Those that succeed win more students and their fees. Those that fail lose their students and go bankrupt as they rightfully should.

Having furnished parents with the choice to send their child anywhere they want, we must overcome the obstacle that prevents them doing so already - money. This is imperative if we are to create a policy that ensures a universally available education. In a freely privatized and competitive school system we can be sure that standards will inevitably improve and the prospects for those children that attend will be greatly increased. However, privatized schools charge fees for the education they deliver and there will be a large minority of children in the nation who will be unable to attend. Their parents simply won't be able to afford the costs, thus the all-important factor of *accessibility* must be dealt with.

The solution to this problem is one in which government can play a useful and vital role, but not to the extent of sabotaging the educational experiences of our nation's children. In order to ensure that high quality education is universally available to all children within an environment of a competitive school system, the government must provide a *scholarship voucher* to each and every child. Every single child in the country would receive a scholarship that amounts to a certain value. The value will be set by the Ministry of Education at an amount that pays for a robust education at a good private school for a period of a term or a year. At the end of the duration of the scholarship, it would be automatically renewed for the same or greater value and accounting for inflation.

Critically, these scholarships will be redeemable at any educational institution regardless of whether it is a conventional or religious madrasah school, provided that the institution conforms to minimum standards set by the Ministry of Education. The choice of where to send their child will lie entirely at the discretion of parents where it rightfully should be. If parents wish to redeem their scholarship at a school that charges fees greater than the value of the scholarship, then parents will have to supply the balance.

At the same time, the government must transitionally cede control of its own schools and institutions over a period of time by selling them or leasing their facilities to private sector educators at market rates. This may result in a hue and cry from socialist shills and agitators, but we should not be concerned when taking these schools out of government hands. They have failed, and we must be ruthlessly pragmatic.

Surely every single one of our children, rich or poor, deserves the highest quality schooling possible. Therefore, it is not economically, commercially or socially responsible to pursue a policy that subsidizes schools that are consistently failing the children who attend them. Children only get one chance at a childhood and just one chance for a decent education. We simply cannot continue to prop up failing schools.

The savings from State school closures would be placed back into the fund from which the scholarships are drawn. By moving away from ownership and operational control of schools and towards funding and regulation, the savings would be enormous, and the system would become more transparent. For the same levels of expenditure, the power of the market would achieve significantly better results. The taxpayer will get more 'bang for their buck', and the result will be a universally accessible system with no child excluded.

One advantage of this system is that it would entirely eliminate the two tiered system of poor Urdu-medium government schools and excellent English-medium private schools. Even the poorest child in the country would have the opportunity to benefit from an excellent English-medium education. This would stop the increasing and debilitating social stratification of society and the unfair advantages in job-seeking by those who benefit from an English-medium experience.

Naturally, parents who still wished to send their child to an Urdu-medium institution or a madrasah would retain that right. There would be no compulsion in the matter, but the value of the scholarship would be set at the average amount that a good English-medium school requires. Although much maligned by their critics, and often unfairly, madrasah schools currently provide an excellent way for children to receive religious instruction in a cost effective manner. Some charge few or no fees. If anything, by co-opting such schools into the overall system, their performance and standards will only improve and they will move into the mainstream as viable schools that provide a comprehensive education.

In effect, instead of the government spending taxpayer's money mindlessly on tangibles such as school buildings, textbooks and pencils that only have a marginal connection with the quality of a child's education, they would be investing funds *directly* into the child's education. The schools themselves would be left to worry about operational minutiae, and they would be well incentivised to perform. Remember, if they failed their students and dissatisfied their parents, a school would run the risk of being closed down from a lack of fee income as parents withdraw their children and enrol them elsewhere. They would simply switch schools, and the *scholarship voucher* would switch with them. In this system, the money follows the children.

Pakistan's mass educational system would be further revolutionized with a long overdue overhaul of a national *curriculum* that places Pakistan, its history, language, ideology and mission at the centre of school life. We are encountering countless problems today because our youth have little or no idea about our history and the sacrifices that were made to bring Pakistan into being. They have no idea of their role in the Ummah and the high standards that are expected of them. Neither do they learn of the richness of our major languages, Urdu, Persian and Arabic. As Allama Iqbal said, *"the individual is firm by nation's coherence, otherwise nothing, the wave is only in the ocean, and outside it is nothing."* We must finally discard our infatuation with Westernisation and instead restore the visionary ideology of Allama Iqbal to our classrooms, colleges and campuses. Pakistan is an Ideological State based on the Holy Qur'an and the Sunnah. It is time to re-declare our independence.

Under the proposals here, if the national education budget were steered towards 'subsidizing schooling instead of schools', the government could no longer be accused of being the problem rather than the solution. There would be little need for red tape, and little room for corruption and the 'ghost' institutions made possible through overwhelming bureaucracy. Government would only need to implement a relatively simple administration procedure to keep track of scholarships and to administer funds to schools when *scholarships vouchers* were redeemed.

The market has already worked wonders in our existing private education sector. All we need do is to make it accessible to all. The system is also flexible. Children with disabilities and special needs would receive *scholarship vouchers* of a higher value appropriate with their needs. They too, rich or poor, would benefit from the high quality education system of their parents choice. The same principle of scholarships would be used equally for the purposes of further and higher education and even adult education.

This is the ideal system. It would be constantly reforming, innovating and delivering for our children. By leveraging the tremendous power of free market competition, the federal schooling budget would be used efficiently and productively. Furthermore, the nation would benefit from a continuous supply of increasingly motivated, well-adjusted and well-educated young people ready to take the nation forward into a bright and prosperous future. By enabling the most disadvantaged young people to benefit from top quality schooling on par with what private sector schools achieve today, society would become truly equitable and fair to all. Not just in socialist utopian visions, but in a very real sense. A simple concept - no child left behind.

5

ON LAW

"Endeavour to obey, O heedless one! Liberty is the fruit of obligation. By duty a man of no worth is made worthy; by disobedience his fire is turned to ashes. Whoso would master the sun and the stars, let him make himself a prisoner of Law!"

Allama Iqbal

The attempt to create a utopia on Earth has been tried countless times in history. If rarely achieved in practice, humanity's imagination knows few bounds; the world's folklore often recounts mythical tales of perfect societies, some that existed, others yet to be created. Amongst all the tales of Camelot, Shangri-La and Zion, lies the idea that a perfect, harmonious order can arise. These concepts exist for a reason; the greater mans apparent progress, the greater his problems seem to multiply. There is universal acknowledgment that every society in existence today is lacking in some way - all fall short, no matter how pristine the veneer of civilization. It seems there is a sense of longing for better days. And what is politics anyway, if not an attempt by certain idealistic souls to nudge a flawed society closer to a notion of perfection?

A problem arises. The writer Thomas Fuller wrote, *"A fool's paradise is a wise man's hell."* Utopia lies in the eye of the beholder and there is no universally acceptable version. For

53

those unbelievers unconvinced by the notion of a spiritual nirvana, the model to be followed must chime with the alleged certainty of science. And so we witness a succession of 'isms' to that end: anarchism, socialism, Maoism, fascism, Marxism, libertarianism and countless others, each more 'scientifically proven' than the next. The only common points between these pseudo-scientific concoctions are first, they are all Western in origin, and second, in their conclusion: an idealistic society that runs in clockwork fashion, where all former wrongs and oppressions are righted and justice and harmony reign supreme.

The problem is that in their methods these ideologies are all plagued by the same sense of *moral relativism*. With petty opinion supreme and divine law abandoned, there is no fixed, absolute sense of morality - the leaders alone decide what is right and wrong. Inevitably, the priority to do what is 'right' for society quickly mutates into doing what is 'right' for the leadership. The masses are soon forgotten, and the leaders quickly become self-absorbed and primarily interested in consolidating their own power. In the meantime, the masses are buried in an avalanche of political, social, spiritual and economic injustices. The propaganda may be ubiquitous, but as millions of souls rack up as 'collateral damage', the victims may fail to see the point.

Of course, we never arrive at the perfected destination, but that was probably never the intent. For the cannier amongst us, we may realize that for the leaders of these movements, often the destination is only a fiction, just a mirage in the desert, never to be attained, always to be postponed. The conjured light at the end of the tunnel is only there for show, unreachable, but highly desirable, just enough to convince the long-suffering masses to take a few more steps. The copious flow of misinformation, half-truths and blatant truths spewed and echoed by our leaders and their shills constitute the script in this theatrical circus.

Propaganda is powerful. Through artificially manufactured consent, and the sanctification of Westernization at the expense of our traditional values, we can be manipulated into willingly ceding control over our own future. Thus in spite of Western philosophies such as socialism, liberalism and democracy having had catastrophic effects on our society, we are continually brainwashed into thinking that this is what we really want. And in the end, in spite of all the vaunted claims, we remain continually stressed, constantly sacrificing, permanently anxious, until one by one, we shuffle off this mortal coil. The vast majority of us were never going to realize the dream.

In faith lies a straighter path. In faith, the journey *is* the destination. In accordance with the commandments of The Almighty, one can immediately realize ones utopia - a state of contentment and satisfaction that no earthly force can shatter. For unlike the secular path, where materially, morally and spiritually, there is no peace of mind, here, if you seek to please God, He in His mercy, will please you. But this notion of utopia can transcend the individual and also encompass society and State. Islamic law provides a moral framework for State governance. It is not theoretical, hypothetical or pseudo-scientific. Divinely inspired, it is a framework which if implemented with wisdom, *can* re-create the societal utopia last seen during the Golden Age of Muslim civilization. All it requires is the faith to make it happen.

In that regard, we in Pakistan have been blessed beyond measure. Westerners abandoned faith a long time ago, but we still value our Islamic creed. However, these values seem to be slowly slipping away. We have wandered from the straight path and into darker territory, a 'terra incognita' that is the product of our own fevered minds. Today, we have joined the *"random caravan without destination,"* that Allama Iqbal once described Western civilization to be. Like the West, we now wander aimlessly and fruitlessly, buffeted by forces beyond our control or comprehension. But unlike the West, we are not destined for oblivion, but for glory. So before we follow the misguided off the edge of the proverbial cliff, we must come to our senses. We must correct our course. We must realize that our salvation does not lie in the limitations of the Occident.

Shakespeare once wrote *"This above all: to thine own self be true..."* By forsaking truth, we have stripped ourselves of identity, purpose and direction. We have made ourselves helpless and vulnerable to internal and external threats. Perceiving that we can do nothing of ourselves, so despairing are we that many of us have given up the ghost of initiative. Many just sit idly, awaiting the Messiah. It is thought that only the sheer force of his personality will break our chains. Yet we delude ourselves. Not that he will not come - he surely will. But that he will bring us something we do not already have, a weapon or tactic that is lacking in our current arsenal.

When our saviour arrives, he will not bring an iota of anything alien, nothing that we will not recognize. We already have the knowledge we need. The Messiah will only come to confirm and implement the law of the Holy Qur'an. Yes, the very same book that just now sits on a bookshelf near you. Except this time, its light will not be confined to within its pages and to the heart of its reader, but to all places where it has not yet reached. Its pages will be opened, and its light will spread, house by house, street by street, market by market, city by city, and country by country. It will not remain a prisoner to dusty shelves but will be liberated to the corridors of political power, the offices of state, and the courts of all the lands. *Then* the world will rejoice in utopia.

In the meantime, this Muslim Camelot eludes us, and not because the Messiah has yet to arrive, but because we remain crippled by our own arrogance. Although we could achieve our Eden on Earth tomorrow if we wished it, we suffer from a mass delusion, a misguided belief that it is not beyond the wit of mere mortals to devise and regulate a system of law capable of solving our problems. We have placed our Islamic inheritance in cold storage while trying almost every Western ideological concoction, all to no avail. As a result, we have short-changed ourselves and postponed the new glorious dawn.

By forsaking a divine gift, our strength has been sapped and our enemies emboldened. Once we commanded the world - now we are left begging to it on our knees. All the while, the answer to our problems was in front of our eyes. Let us now recognize ourselves as faithful servants of God by finally allowing His divine law to uplift us, as is its purpose. Regardless of stripe or sect, we are Muslims. Pakistan was founded as a Muslim-majority state with Islam as its ideology. Let us now gently remind each other: *"to thine own self be true..."*

* * * * *

Why have we been conditioned into believing that Shariah is an obsolete aspect of Islam? Why are we told to treat this system of law with such contempt? Why are those who advocate it labelled obscurantist and fundamentalist? Reality check - without Shariah, there would have been no Muslim civilization, no Islamic Golden Age, no exquisite mosques in far flung corners of the world and no teeming masses standing in the ranks of Muslim brotherhood. Without Shariah, there would have been no House of Wisdom in Baghdad, no scientific heights in Muslim Spain and no glorious reign of Mughal dynasties in India. There would have been no heroic Ottoman exploits, no sprawling trade routes and no rich cultural marvels. Where would the world have been then?

Let us remember that the malaise that affects the Muslim world today did not come to pass until relatively recently. For over a thousand years Muslim civilization prospered and flourished. The brutal dictatorships, autocratic monarchies and corrupt social democracies that plague us today did not exist. There was no tyranny or power-mongering, because under rule-of-law governments, rulers a few hundred years ago were obliged by the law of Shariah to protect and preserve the legal rights of the people and to be clearly seen to be doing so.

These rights, known as 'huqooq-ul-ibaad' or 'the rights of man,' had to be upheld by all rulers under the supervision of the scholarly classes and included basic natural entitlements such as the right to life, liberty, legal process and protection from State oppression and undue coercion. Any ruler that denied the people these rights would fall out of favour with the Ulema and his moral authority would be compromised. This lack of religious cover would then leave him wide open to challenges to his leadership. It was a stable yet flexible model that provided a useful balance of power and a check on unrestricted tyranny.

The wide application of Shariah allowed for the administration and maintenance of justice for all. Even during times of political turmoil, when power transitions were often disorderly and violent, the scholars were agents of consistency and stability. Through the law, they upheld divine injunctions elaborated on in the Holy Qur'an and Sunnah of the Noble Prophet (peace be upon him). They delivered speedy and fair decisions on matters great and small and were instrumental in protecting property rights and the right to conduct one's life and business as one pleased.

There is no doubt that the Shariah and its scholars were absolutely essential to the outstanding success that Islamic civilization enjoyed from its inception into the 19th century. Whereas now religious teaching and instruction is maligned and ridiculed, back then it was seen as the ultimate career choice for aspiring youngsters. The Ulema of yesteryear were widely respected and admired in society. Today though, the Islamic jurists who once wielded so much influence have been replaced by a system of English Common law and the Shariah has been pushed to the extreme margins of our legal system. For decades, the villains, spoilers and chancers in power have been complicit in what seems a canny strategy inherited from the British.

When the British toppled the last vestiges of the Mughal dynasty, Shariah law had been the first to go. The British found it unacceptable as it represented too great a symbol of independent freedom and justice - this being totally contrary to their policy of violent imperial subjugation. However, the British were clever enough to realize that it would be expedient to throw the subject peoples a few morsels here and there to give the impression of benevolence. To placate the Muslims who had lived with Islamic law for hundreds of years, the Raj kept the Shariah courts running but heavily restricted them to handling only minor family law cases. Using these courts as a valve for jettisoning the frustrations of the devout, they could then control and monitor the extent and reach of the Islamic opposition.

The imperialists are long gone, but incredibly, today in Pakistan, Shariah courts still only administer family law - a tiny subset of their original historical jurisdiction. The 'brown-sahib' successors of the British performed beyond the wildest expectations of the old imperial motherland: the phrase, 'more Catholic than the Pope,' springs to mind. Whereas the constitution they created contains slogans that declare Shariah to be *"the source of law,"* if this were even slightly true, today we would not witness the astounding levels of injustices perpetrated on the innocent in our country. Now our shameful judges administer two laws - one for the rich and famous, and another for everyone else. Needless to say, the latter is far less permissive.

It is an open conspiracy. To this day, preferring the 'legal' freedom to loot and pillage the nation at will, the judiciary and political elite cannot allow Shariah to gain ground, and so they marginalize it through propaganda and misinformation. In the media it is portrayed as reactionary and anachronistic, only defended by shouting, wild-eyes mullahs. We are told by the ultra-liberal media that the world has moved on and that we should adapt and get with the times. If 'adapting' means suffering under a morally, spiritually and socially bankrupt Western legal system, they can think again.

One would not think it, but the Pakistani constitution claims that the State must govern, *"...in accordance with the teachings and requirements of Islam as set out in the Holy Qur'an and Sunnah..."* This is ironic, since the final arbiters of the law, the Supreme Court justices, tend to be more knowledgeable about Latin legalese than the intricacies of Shariah. How it could be possible for Judges to ensure that the nations laws align with Shariah if they are not even schooled in it is not explained. What it does explain is the failure of this judicial system to even conform to common sense let alone administer justice to the people.

On paper, on issues where Islamic law does not provide clear direction, our democratically chosen legislature is supposed to use its discretion to adopt laws informed by Islamic values. The so-called "repugnancy clause," mandates that a judicial body (the Federal Shariat Court) can overturn any law repugnant to Islam. Thus in principle, the National Assembly can only pass legislation if it reflects the 'spirit' of Islamic law. The problem is that never mind controversial matters where there is no precedent or clarity, on matters where Shariah *does* provide a clear lead, it is ignored entirely.

For example, irrespective of affiliation, can we all agree that interest based lending is illegal under Shariah? The Holy Qur'an is crystal clear and any Muslim of any stripe will agree. Yet regardless of the clear illegality, our apparently 'Shariah-infused' legal system ironically condones the State Bank of Pakistan setting base interest rates as monetary policy which the Holy Qur'an tells us is akin to it declaring war on Allah and His Messenger (peace be upon him). Why we would allow a legal system to preside over us that defies Allah and His Messenger (peace be upon him) in such a wilful manner is a matter that is beyond my personal comprehension. But perhaps this is what happens when men are allowed to make up the rules in their own interest while using Islam as mere adornment.

Shariah is permanent and absolute. There is no moral relativism involved. It is neither subject to 'constitutional suspensions' nor tolerant of 'National Reconciliation Ordinances'. Properly implemented, it is not just a set of legal rules like any other. Being of divine origin, it is something far deeper and higher, infused with perfect moral and metaphysical purpose. At its very core, Shariah represents the concept of fairness, justice and equality that illuminates every aspect of the Islamic way of life. Inherent is the idea that all people, and all governments are subject to justice under the law.

True Shariah applies to all, rulers *and* ruled, a notion that would be highly inconvenient to the current villains in power. And true enough, our leaders do not fear any vaunted Supreme Court justice as much as they fear the Shariah. Not surprising, as under a Shariah system they would be the first to be called to account. The status quo would lose everything if the penetrating light of divinely inspired law were ever to be shone in their guilty faces. Shariah is not a system of law that can be amended or distorted according to the whims and fashions of the time. No wonder they despise it.

Many naysayers argue that the Muslim world is too divided to even agree on what the Shariah is, but this is not true. There are only a tiny minority of issues that actually create controversy. Regardless of affiliation, all Muslims will agree, for example, that Shariah prohibits lending money at interest, consuming alcohol, paying or taking bribes, slandering the innocent, appropriating the property of others or bearing false witness. Even for liberal interpreters of the faith, these matters are not in dispute. Others argue that some punishments associated with Shariah seem harsh to their liberal sensibilities. Yet even if these punishments were as 'unjust' as they claim, they would pale in comparison to the sheer magnitide of the injustices currently suffered by many millions of our fellow citizens due to the vagaries of permissive Western law and its inadequate punishments.

Ever since our leaders adopted Westernism root and branch, they now only pay lip service to the faith of our forefathers. Empty slogans and platitudes are the only thing on offer, ostensibly to placate the maulvis and mullahs. But the shoddy legal system they continue to defend is clearly broken. It is untenable, unworkable, and unconscionable - a national laughing stock rather than an institution worthy of respect. The people demand change. The Greek philosopher Heraclitus once said, *"If it were not for injustice, men would not know justice."* Well by now, the Pakistani people have suffered enough injustice to know what justice looks like. For the masses, the return of Shariah is highly popular. They know it is the only way the feckless leaders who rule over us can be called to account for their evils.

Our leaders have paramount responsibility to fulfil the divine injunction to *"command the right and prohibit the wrong."* It is time for them to either realize their responsibilities or get out of the way. For far too long they have constructed a fluid moral universe around us where the goal posts of right and wrong are constantly being moved. There is no excuse for such travesties of justice. Can we not understand that a legal system that absolves the most heinous crimes for the sake of political expediency is worse than junk?

A legal system that produces trash like the 'National Reconciliation Ordinance' is an affront to the dignity of the nation and a slap in the face of the millions who fought and died for it. This is just not good enough. We need to live by a higher law, a set of unchanging principles that order life in accordance with the will of God. Shariah is a law that applies equally to every person, great or small, ruler or ruled. No one can be above it and all are bound by it.

As believers in "there is no God but Allah," we must dispense with all the idols that take us away from His straight path. That means abolishing this rotten legal detritus the British left behind and which passes for a legal system, and establishing one in which Allah and His Messenger (peace be upon him) set the ground rules. Arrogance and willful rebellion led to the downfall of Satan. Is this the fate we want? Allah did not wrong Satan, he wronged himself. There is a lesson in that perhaps, for those who reflect.

7

ON MONEY

"Lenin is said to have declared that the best way to destroy the Capitalist System was to debauch the currency... Lenin was certainly right... By a continuing a process of inflation, governments can confiscate, secretly and unobserved, an important part of the wealth of their citizens.... There is no subtler, no surer means of overturning the existing basis of society... The process engages all the hidden forces of economic law on the side of destruction, and does it in a manner which not one man in a million is able to diagnose."

John Maynard Keynes

A corrupt and insidious scheme is being perpetrated on the Pakistani people. It affects the lives of every single member of society bar none, and yet it is something that is unknown, unquestioned and unheard of. It is the morally bankrupt monetary system that is equivalent to legalised counterfeiting. It is our national currency: a currency based on the mere promise of a cabal of elite bankers, who, by cranking a few simple policy levers can unilaterally condemn millions to financial hardship and misery.

There is a clear link to be found between a nation's living standards and the inherent value of its currency. We have thousands of years of history from which to draw lessons. Many civilisations have risen and fallen, yet the demise of every single one ran in direct parallel with the inevitable debasement of its money by emperors and princelings. They would do this by adulterating gold and silver coins by adding a small percentage of base metals, leading not only to a decline in their value but also a decline in public confidence.

The modern equivalent of this long held tradition is to inflate the money supply through the excessive printing of arbitrary paper money. Consider how we must endure the hidden tax on our wealth via the systematic inflation of the Rupee which inevitably degrades its value. This debasement continues to be often deliberate and systematic; and done in order to pay for populist welfare, aggressive wars and to subsidize special interests. The result of this policy always leads to decline and stagnation. It is inevitable. Historically, whenever governments indulged in monetary inflation to serve their own ends, it led to the weakening if not eventual destruction of their economies.

When money is created out of thin air and without the backing of some commodity like gold or silver, there are extra coins or notes circulating in the economy that are chasing the same quantity of goods. This results in the excess money manifesting itself in a general increase in the level of prices (price inflation). More money in the economy does not necessarily mean more wealth. What matters is the 'buying power' of that money, or how many goods and services can be bought with it.

Every extra Rupee issued into circulation which is not backed by a commodity slightly reduces the buying power of the rest of the notes in circulation, devaluing them. When the supply of money is increased in this way the welfare of ordinary people is damaged because the resulting price inflation causes all wealth and savings to lose value. Effectively, it is a surreptitious tax on all holders of cash, deposits, savings or investments in society (everyone) - a tax imposed by the money-issuing central bank.

Yet for thousands of years, it was only gold and silver that was used as the money of choice. Both gold and silver are durable, precious, and widely accepted: a near perfect store of wealth and exchange mechanism. Come war, famine or pestilence, they always held their value and indeed they still do. Many paper currencies have come and gone, but these metals are still considered precious and valuable.

In ancient Rome, before the era of chaotic inflation when base metals were introduced into the coinage, a gold aureus coin spent in a market would buy a quality toga, a belt and a pair of good sandals. The comparison is crude, but today, the equivalent amount of gold will buy a quality suit, belt and a pair of good dress shoes. Thus gold has not depreciated in its purchasing power in the intervening two thousand years. Compare that record to the modern currencies that sometimes lose their purchasing power precipitously in just a few weeks. Compare it to the Pakistani Rupee's continuous slide in value since Independence.

Clearly, gold holds its worth, and so backed by gold, currencies are inherently more honest, sound and stable. Gold backed currencies maintain their value because the money supply can only be expanded with the acquisition of more gold, and the amount of money in the economy can only expand from the increased production and wealth that is created by productive hard work and the fruits of capital investment. The money supply cannot be increased on a politician's whim - only through honest effort.

When all paper money was backed by gold or silver, as in the early days of the GB pound, the US dollar and the Swiss franc, inflation in those nations was practically nil. Under a gold or silver standard, nations prospered in wealth and made huge inroads into eliminating poverty. There are clear historical parallels. The rise of great civilisations was made possible by their establishment of widely accepted and honest currency. The early Romans held sway over the world with their silver denarius, the Byzantines with their bezant, the Muslims with dinars and dirhams, and the British with their pounds sterling. Today it is the American dollar that has gained monetary supremacy, but just like their imperial predecessors, the Americans have fallen into the trap of monetary inflation.

For political leaders, it has always been a tempting trap to fall into. There came a time in the histories of all the great empires when their growing governments sought to be rid of the fiscal discipline that the gold or silver standard imposed. As stated by American congressman Ron Paul, *"Because gold is honest money, it is disliked by dishonest men."* Thus for centuries, inflation and debt have been used by tyrants of all stripes to consolidate power, promote aggression, and provide 'bread and circuses' for the people. They found the restrictions commodity money imposed on them to be highly inconvenient. After all, why choose between 'guns and butter', when you can clip the coinage and have both?

By the 11th century, Islamic influence, trade and practice extended far and wide across three continents. Muslim merchants dominated trade for thousands of miles in every direction from Arabia. Islam spread widely as Muslim merchants travelled throughout the world. The nature of how their commerce was to be conducted was crystal clear: *"O my people! Give just measure and weight, and do not deprive people of what is rightfully theirs by diminishing the value of their things and do not commit evil in the land with intent to corrupt and destroy..."(The Holy Qur'an, 11:85).* The strength and honest nature of the Muslim gold dinar was decisive in spreading Islamic civilisation. Backed by an exact and unchanging weight (no less than 4.25 grams), the gold dinars coined by the Caliphate were gladly and readily accepted everywhere.

They represented sound and honest money and a measure of value that held its integrity over time and could be trusted. They were a positive reflection of the honest merchants who traded them and the faith that they practiced. This helped to spread the influence of Islam and did so where no armies could possibly have reached: places like the Indonesian archipelago, West Africa and Western China.

But after the last real dinar was minted and the stability of the currency was spoiled by debasement, trade and commerce went into decline. Thanks to the elaborate spending excesses of ruling sultans and caliphs, the bi-metallic gold and silver standard was heavily compromised and then eventually abandoned. It is no coincidence that Muslim civilisation fell into disarray when its leaders debased the dinar. Led astray from Qur'anic wisdom, confidence fell, trade spluttered to a halt, and the vast bulk of the people fell into the ravages of poverty and tyranny. Truly, Islamic civilization has never recovered since.

With Muslim decline, it was Western Europe that took on the gold mantle. And with their adoption of sound and honest money came enormous success. In the 18th century the major west European nations adopted the gold standard. Capitalising on private property rights and free markets, they grew rapidly in influence and prosperity. They went on to conquer, carving out vast empires with many weakened Muslim nations falling under their imperial grip. An up-and-coming colonial power, Britain, grew to hold massive swathes of territory in the New World of the Americas. There in 1776, protesting to 'taxation without representation' and the belligerent behaviour of British troops, a small band of revolutionaries gathered in Philadelphia in the colony of Pennsylvania to declare their independence from the English crown.

A few years later, victorious from their war of liberation, many of these men gathered to discuss and compose the constitution of the new nation. As the debate turned to the new monetary system, there was general agreement on what must be done. Being worldly-wise and historically literate, they knew the pitfalls of a non-backed paper currency. Their familiarity with the subject was illuminated by their own personal experiences. They could not easily forget the hyper-inflation they had endured only a few years previously under the erstwhile 'Continental dollar' when the governors of the colonies had printed paper money excessively causing skyrocketing inflation and entrenching the deep poverty of the colonists. (Even today, the phrase 'not worth a Continental' is still heard in America when describing something of no value).

Thomas Jefferson later noted in his correspondence, *"Paper is poverty,... it is only the ghost of money, and not money itself... the trifling economy of paper, as a cheaper medium, or its convenience for transmission, weighs nothing in opposition to the advantages of the precious metals... it is liable to be abused, has been, is, and forever will be abused, in every country in which it is permitted."*

Wisely understanding the need for honesty and confidence in the new currency, the Founding Fathers expressly decreed in their new constitution that all legal tender would be coined and backed with gold and silver. They made no provision for a paper money-issuing central bank, with some noting that it would only eventually be hijacked by special interests and become an instrument of profiteering, economic tyranny and plunder.

A few years later however, a central bank was briefly created only to be abolished soon after. While it lasted, Jefferson was bitterly opposed, warning, *"I believe that [central] banking institutions are more dangerous than standing armies... The banks... have the regulation of the safety-valves of our fortunes, and... condense and explode them at their will..."* James Madison spoke out against the corporate interests and usurers who sought to usurp the money supply, *"History shows that the money changers have used every form of abuse, intrigue, deceit and violent means possible to maintain control over governments by controlling the money and the issuance of it."*

With the abolition of the US central bank again in 1836 the link to gold was restored. Over the next decades, combined with classical liberal economic policies and limited government, the new nation, conceived in liberty, underwent one of the greatest economic rises in history. The American economy grew and industrialized rapidly, surpassing every other industrial nation and becoming the pre-eminent world power.

Based on US productivity and military might, the dollar soon replaced the British Pound to become the world's currency of choice. But in 1913, prior to the outbreak of the First World War, American politicians backed by powerful Zionist banking dynasties such as the *Rothschilds, Warburgs, Morgans and Rockefellers*, succeeded in creating the Federal Reserve System, a central bank whose practices were contrary to the spirit and letter of the US Constitution and the wishes of the Founding Fathers. The new system meant that the Federal Reserve Bank could print money at will to finance ever increasing government expenditures and warfare. No-one recalled the chilling words of the founder of the powerful Rothschild dynasty: *"Give me control over a nation's currency, and I care not who makes its laws"*. The link to gold was thus compromised - the banking interests had taken over.

It was the ensuing Federal Reserve monetary inflation that fuelled the economic boom of the 1920's. Interest rates (the cost of money) were kept artificially low, and the money printing machines worked non-stop. What resulted was a scramble as individuals and business misdirected capital into unwise projects and gorged themselves on cheap credit. Over in Europe, the German equivalent of the Federal Reserve, the Reichsbank, took monetary policy to new heights of insanity. Hyperinflation became rampant as German workers took their wages home in wheelbarrows filled with worthless currency. It couldn't last. In 1929, the bubble finally burst, sparking the Wall Street Crash and the Great Depression that was to persist until 1939. The tens of millions who suffered understandably blamed the free market and 'greedy capitalists'. But as the tide of despair swept Adolf Hitler into power in Germany, little did the world know that the real cause of its agonies was Central Bank chicanery.

In reality, the market had never been 'free' at all. It had been the Fed's imprudent policy of inflation designed to expand the power of the corporate moneyed interests that had resulted in the boom. And it worked. Conveniently for the Zionists, the ensuing bust and contraction wiped out thousands of small and medium sized private independent banks all over the country. This only further consolidated the hold of the major banking families over the world's money markets.

The influence of these special interests went deep. Still, suspicious of a future return to gold, in 1933 they were able to lobby the legislature to confiscate all gold from the economy, making it illegal for Americans to hold, buy or sell gold. This removed all restraints on the Fed to inflate for war and welfare. These banking interests through their influence of the 'independent' US central bank were then able to profiteer from the colossal borrowing requirements of the US government when it needed to re-arm and fund the massively expensive war effort around the world against the axis powers. Not to mention the huge costs of post-war reconstruction.

After the Second World War, with empires in ruins and entire regions devastated, America had secured its dominance on all fronts. The Zionist banking families could now call the shots worldwide. At the post-war Bretton Woods conference in 1945, the world's central bankers engineered a newfangled inflationary monetary system in which they would sever their own links to gold and peg their currencies to the US dollar if America 'promised' to link the dollar to gold.

Ever since, in order to maintain this peg with the dollar, a central bank must purchase US treasuries and thus expand its credit supply to keep the domestic currency at par. Central banks, banking on America's apparent stability and prosperity, thus accumulate massive reserves of dollars in order to make their exchange rates more favourable for exports. However, the people who actually pay for this profligacy are not central bankers, but rather anyone with denominated assets in the domestic currency. Thus the average domestic consumer witnesses inflation first hand when the price of everything inexorably rises.

After Bretton Woods, every newly independent nation established central banks. Emulating the Federal Reserve and Bank of England, all were to use interest-rate manipulation and inflation as a policy tool. In 1948, Quaid-e-Azam inaugurated the 'State Bank of Pakistan', however, unlike his contemporaries, he was wise to the threat that Central Banking systems posed. He had no intention of Pakistan ever following the Western economic model and its central bank being used as a source of inflation and pauperisation.

In what turned out to be his final speech before his death, he laid out his views emphatically, stating that the State Bank of Pakistan must evolve *"banking practices compatible with Islamic ideas of social and economic life. The economic system of the West has created almost insoluble problems for humanity and to many of us it appears that only a miracle can save it from disaster that is facing the world. It has failed to do justice between man and man and to eradicate friction from the international field. On the contrary, it was largely responsible for the two world wars in the last half-century."*

"The Western world, in spite of its advantages, of mechanization and industrial efficiency is today in a worse mess than ever before in history. The adoption of Western economic theory and practice will not help us in achieving our goal of creating a happy and contended people. We must work our destiny in our own way and present to the world an economic system based on true Islamic concept of equality of manhood and social justice. We will thereby be fulfilling our mission as Muslims and giving to humanity the message of peace which alone can save it and secure the welfare, happiness and prosperity of mankind. May the State Bank of Pakistan prosper and fulfil the high ideals which have been set as its goal."

While Quaid-e-Azam made his awe-inspiring intentions clear, he passed away only two months later, leaving Pakistan's fate in the hands of lesser mortals. His successors were not as perceptive as he was. Kowtowing to Western practice, the government of Pakistan entrusted the State Bank to unaccountable elites who henceforth mismanaged the issuance of money. To this day, Quaid-e-Azam's State Bank has yet to be liberated from their clutches. Meanwhile, the US dollars link to gold became increasingly tenuous until finally in 1971, it was quietly discarded by Richard Nixon. Since then the dollar floats free and is purely a political currency, un-backed by gold, silver or anything else. No currency in the world is now sustainable, not even the Pakistani Rupee.

What we have seen since is a gigantic worldwide dollar bubble and the globalizing of inflation. Over the decades America has had the most to gain from this devious system. Because the world accepts dollars as if they were gold, America has only had to 'counterfeit' more paper dollars, spend them overseas, allow them to be lent back to Americans by foreign central banks and enjoy unearned prosperity.

The central bankers in Europe, China, the oil rich Middle East, Japan and the developing world who accumulated US dollars and sold America their goods and services in exchange for paper dollars were only too keen to loan those dollars back to them. This allowed America to export its inflation and delay the consequences that we now are starting to witness. Debt is literally America's largest export as foreign banks and sovereign wealth funds have amassed trillions of increasingly worthless dollars. This is the unholy revenue stream that funds American Imperial adventurism from 'sea to shining sea'.

History will inevitably repeat itself. We still live in an age where the dollar is the reserve currency and still favoured by most central banks, but this will not last. Soon international goodwill will run out and the political dollar will fall by the wayside. Creaking under 'imperial overstretch', oddly willing to spark further conflicts, and deeply indebted to East Asian economies to the tune of trillions of dollars, the US is living far beyond its means and unless it changes its policies it is destined to soon live below its means. Through printing money to pay for wars of aggression, corporate welfare and its enormous national debt liability, the status of the dollar will soon be challenged.

The signs are already appearing. Recently the dollar has depreciated rapidly against other currencies as the world is becoming increasingly concerned about America's extravagantly expensive wars and fiscal excesses. As central banks around the world wake up to the relative weakening of the American Imperium, they will surely question why they hold the bulk of their wealth in dollars; wealth which is shrinking with every cent the dollar slides. At the time of writing, the dollar's decline already amounts to the biggest default in history, having wiped far more off the value of the assets of foreigners than anything else. The world is losing confidence.

Just as other empires throughout history abandoned gold and silver and then fell into decline and were overtaken, it seems that the United States is following a well worn path. Since resorting to inflationary policies, there is little future for the dollar or any dollar denominated assets. But because every other nation, without exception, is inflating too and therefore destroying its own monetary base, the inevitable future crunch will not be confined to America - it will spread far and wide.

This includes Pakistan. Ever since 1948, with the creation of the State Bank of Pakistan, the policy of the government has been to arbitrarily manipulate the money supply, cause inflation, and debase the value of the Rupee. Ironically, the word Rupee is based on an Indo-Aryan word for silver. But silver is valuable, paper money backed by nothing is not.

In violation of the expressed wishes of Quaid-eAzam, the State Bank now bows to the creed of 'Western Inflationary Capitalism'. As a result, through its systematic monetary inflation, the Pakistani masses have seen what little wealth they have simply eroding away. The results are tragically clear. The purchasing power of the Rupee today is only 5 *percent* of what it was in 1947. You would need 20 times as many Rupees to buy the same bundle of goods that could have been bought in 1947. Priced in gold, the goods are not worth any more now than they were then. It's just that the paper notes that buy them are worth a lot less.

This is shocking. Indeed, it is a criminal and dishonest undertaking on a massive scale. It is no surprise then that poverty is so rampant and prosperity is so elusive for so many. The inevitable rising prices that result from extravagant monetary inflation mean that the common man must keep running to simply stand still. The poorest have no chance at all. The system is morally reprehensible. The government hardly needs to worry about taxation or borrowing to fund its extravagances. It is able to finance massive expansions in its interventionist activity by simply printing money.

As any competent economist will agree, inflation, or the general rise in the price level for the goods and services in an economy, is always the result of an increase in the money supply, either encouraged or initiated by government action. There are few other reasons for prices to rise, other than the government interfering in the market system or by the central bank issuing increasing amounts of money and credit. In fact, it is the natural inclination for prices to go down in a competitive free market economy. But this is not allowed to happen.

Paper money that is backed by nothing and created at the whim of bankers and politicians and ardently supported by socialists and pseudo-intellectuals is known as 'fiat money'. It is money that is produced and multiplied through fractional reserve banking systems and which allows the free and easy creation of funds without the political problems associated with taxation or borrowing. The resulting inflation is an appalling scourge on the poorest and most vulnerable in society. It drastically reduces their already low purchasing power by reducing the amount of goods and services that can be bought with what little money they posses. Let's be clear. It is a little understood fact that monetary inflation transfers money from the wealthy to the poor.

How does this happen? Quite simply, when new money is printed or issued in the form of credit, the beneficiaries are those with *direct* credit lines with the government - cronies, the banking-industrial complex, subsidised and well-connected corporations, and politicians. They are issued with newly created money first and are able to buy at the older, lower prices. Newly created, the money has not yet circulated through the economy causing a general rise in price levels. Their 'purchasing power' is thus increased.

Those who suffer are those who see the money at the end of the money chain - the poor and middle classes who only just scrape by when crushed by the inflation and price rises that result from the printing. By the time they get to spend it, the money has circulated or 'trickled' through the economy and is now worth less as prices have risen. By this time, the purchasing power of the same note has been decreased and standard of living of ordinary families has been reduced.

It is the biggest rip-off of all time; an instrument that transfers wealth from the unsuspecting poor and middle classes to the well-healed and well-connected. It is a tragedy that the people who suffer most from their depreciating money do not even understand that it is not natural, but artificial and deliberate. Their honest, hard earned wealth is being surreptitiously stolen from them while the people who promote and safeguard the fiat monetary system benefit exclusively.

The consequences of this system, which has been in place since the birth of the nation are too colossal to possibly measure. The wealth of every single person depreciates through this fiat monetary system. In spite of a solid growth rate that has been maintained on average at around 5% per year for decades, the country remains indebted and poor, and the poorest just get poorer. And yet we still wonder why. For six decades in Pakistan, inflation has been rampant, averaging annually at around 6%. Prices rise when they should be dropping, and the only wealth that we think we have has only resulted in the form of artificially created credit bubbles that have indebted tens of millions across the land and sucked them into a morally bankrupt interest-based loan system. It is a total fraud.

Inflation is felt by everyone but understood by very few. Yet this system has caused colossal amounts of wealth to be transferred from the poor and middle-classes to powerful banks, special interests and favoured industries. Every person acutely discerns that year on year the value of the money in their pockets becomes significantly less and less. But what do we expect when the value of our Rupee lies not in the value of gold or silver as it should, but rather in blind trust in the decisions of a cabal of greasy bankers and politicians? The Rupee, just like the United States dollar is a mere political currency. The trust has now been completely broken. The politicians and central bankers entrusted with the safekeeping of our money have betrayed us.

As wage increases tend to lag behind inflation, ordinary people see their purchasing power drastically reduced. As increases in prices outstrip the increase in their wages, they can only purchase fewer things for the same money. This is no accident. The originators of this abhorrent system intended it to be a means to systematically pauperize the middle classes and poor. As Lenin said, *"The way to crush the bourgeoisie is to grind them between the millstones of taxation and inflation."* His pompous yet ominous statement reveals the true face of modern socialism at its most ruthless. At the time of writing, inflation is running completely out of control, rampaging at

25%, destroying lives, wealth, savings and standards of living for many tens of millions of people.

But the chicanery of our central bankers goes deeper. Their Zionist monetary system is also a primary source of the damaging swings of business cycles. As we saw in 1920's America and many times and in many places since, booms are often cheered on by the financial media but are purely the result of excess credit creation by the central bank. The extra money in the economy effectively lowers interest rates (the price of money), giving rise to cheap and easy credit. This fuels economic activity. But it is purely artificial, and is damaging because the manipulation leads to results that soon swing in the opposite direction.

For a real world example, just look at the recent economic and asset price cycle in Pakistan. Just as happened in 1929, the economy 'overheats' in the form of high inflation due to the increased money supply, after which the central bankers often panic and 'tighten' the money supply by restricting credit and raising interest rates. This causes the boom to turn into bust. The economy then contracts. Businesses go under, investments fail and countless people are thrown out of work, causing disruption and heartache to millions of families.

No matter how hard it tries, the central bank can never get the delicate balance between inflation and employment right because its manipulation of interest rates causes 'mal-investment'. These are investment decisions by businesses that are not optimal because interest rates are not at their natural market level. Interest rates have been artificially raised or lowered, so that businesses invest in projects they would not otherwise have entertained, or refrain from investing in projects that would otherwise have made perfect sense.

It is another example of socialistic control, except it extends not merely to the 'commanding heights' of the economy but even to the nature of money itself. How ironic that in spite of the clear evidence to the contrary, this shady currency system is still promoted as being part of the 'public interest'. This is a clear example of how, when the government intervenes where it should not, catastrophic failures occur. Inflation confers no social or economic benefits at all. It merely serves to redistribute money unfairly, distort incentives, and create havoc in the economy. It is an evil, un-Islamic, immoral process that must be stopped.

Governments cannot resist the temptation of having access to free money to bribe demanding voters. But history tells us clearly that when you consider the human flaws that seem to be all too common in politicians and 'independent' central bankers, the result is that no fiat currency like the US dollar or the Pakistani rupee can serve as a stable medium of exchange for very long. Eventually, its value will become so depreciated through inflation that the people's confidence in their dollars and rupees will evaporate. If printed money has no *real* value, then this is merely legalised counterfeiting. We cannot expect the State to be responsible in its actions here. The temptation is too great for them to not abuse the system.

The monetary system is not well understood by the people, so they do not object to it or see it as the problem that it is. But what people must realise is that inflation is the most heinous corruption and fraud of all, because it is the most universally prevalent and damaging. Any fool knows that counterfeit money is not real wealth, and that by indulging in such a practice, you cannot create wealth. It may be exchanged for goods and services but it is not real - it is fake money. Only real production and employment can create wealth in the long term. Deliberate inflationary policies are dishonest and reprehensible. Inflation puts the wealth and savings of the ordinary person at serious risk. It entrenches dishonest practices and will lead to the eventual (and inevitable) destruction of the economy through monetary collapse.

Some claim that inflation is beneficial, and indeed essential, in modern economies. They claim that there should never be a shortage of credit or money and that any such shortages can lead to a recession. But the widely accepted notion that an artificial increase in the supply of money is economically desirable is one of the greatest fallacies of our age. Embraced by kings, emperors, politicians and corrupt bankers alike, this premise is promoted regardless of the destruction of currency after currency, each inflicting incalculable harm and causing social and political turmoil throughout the world. Clearly, just printing 'funny money' creates the political conditions that breeds the vultures and parasitic leeches who feed off the corrupt system and promote it constantly.

Quaid-e-Azam's viewpoint was clearly formed through the prism of the Islamic worldview as Islam clearly recognises the immorality of such a system. As such, Shariah explicitly forbids the giving and taking of usury. Yet the viability of fiat money is based *entirely* on interest rate manipulations. How shameful then that every government in the Muslim world has opted into a system that bases the foundation of its entire economy on inflation and legalised counterfeiting. So what does it matter then if Islam is the official State religion? How precious is our faith to us if we are willing to sell it for worthless paper rupees? Allama Iqbal specifically warned us against adopting the morally crooked money system of the West. We flaunt divine law at our own peril.

We cannot say that we were not warned. The Noble Prophet (peace be upon him) once said, *"A time is certainly coming over mankind in which there will be nothing (left) that will be of use (or benefit) save a Dinar and a Dirham."* Well, that day of reckoning will soon be upon us. We can continue down the difficult path we have trodden, a path that will eventually lead to economic catastrophe, or we can wake up to the truth of the corruption of the current system. Having ignored the wisdom and prohibitions of the Noble Prophet (peace be upon him) and so become entrapped by our own vanity, we have dug a hole for ourselves from which there is only one escape.

Pakistan must return to a Shariah monetary system that upholds honesty, integrity and justice, a system based on *real* money: gold and silver. Deliberate monetary manipulation and inflation should be clearly rejected by any moralistic society, especially one that espouses honesty, integrity and decent Islamic values. Dishonest money pollutes the entire economic system and breeds a dishonest society. Without sound and honest money, the result is immorality. Yet some still wonder why Pakistan and the rest of the Ummah have not prospered.

Here is a most important point. Let us not forget that gold and silver are not just attractive metals or mere elements in the periodic table. They have an intrinsic, spiritual value assigned by Allah Himself, the Creator and Source of all wealth: *"Behold! Those who disbelieve and die in disbelief, the (whole) Earth full of gold would not be accepted from such a one even if it were offered as ransom..." (The Holy Qur'an 3:91)*. This verse as well as numerous others, remind us that gold (and silver) are likened in the Qur'anic worldview to money - a means of exchange.

The Holy Qur'an goes on to reveal that gold and silver will maintain their status as things of great value in the Hereafter. In other words, gold and silver possess a *spiritual value*, in addition to their physical, worldly value in this material world: *"They are served drinks in silver containers and cups that are translucent. Translucent cups, though made of silver; they rightly deserved all this..." (The Holy Qur'an 76:15-16)*.

Proving beyond doubt that gold has a *metaphysical value* (meta meaning 'beyond', literally: 'beyond physics'), the dinar is also destined to play a very significant role on the Day of Resurrection. In a famous Hadith, the weight of the goodness in a person's heart when measured against a dinar, will be the determination by which the Noble Prophet (peace be upon him) will beseech The Almighty to liberate people from the Hell-fire. Clearly, gold and silver are not ordinary. They have a sacred significance. Nobody can argue against the notion that Allah, in His wisdom, means for the believers to use them as money. It is the only *halal* way. Counterfeit paper money will not suffice.

The use of gold and silver as the Islamic medium of exchange is irrefutable. Our leaders are guilty in having abandoned the glorious legacy of our forefathers in favour or spurious 'funny money'. We have paid, and continue to pay a horrendous price for flouting divine laws. Our leaders, who are responsible, have little or no idea as to the reality of the *haram* money that they continue to peddle to us, nor do they understand the inherent dangers. Unfortunately we are at a stage where the government tolerates and seeks to cover up flagrant abuses. So far though, the prospects of reform are slight. Either the politicians have bought into the system, or they have no idea that they are unwitting participants.

Even trained scholars of Islamic law seem unwilling to disclose the secrets of our fraudulent monetary system, and only a few men of understanding speak out. It seems increasingly obvious that only a profound spiritual revival will spark the concept in the minds of our people of the dangers of our monetary system. We must spread the truth far and wide and publicly denounce non-redeemable paper money as totally unacceptable for a dignified, honourable Islamic ideological State such as Pakistan.

We must bring about the needed consensus that will enable us to reject fiat money and return to commodity based money based fully on silver and gold in order to eradicate inflation and restore public and international confidence in the currency. We must educate people to the dangers and refute the lies and unfounded allegations that it is not the government, but traders and merchants who are responsible for prices hikes.

If we are to finally reject the status quo and actually exercise monetary responsibility, we must abolish the State Bank of Pakistan's monetary manipulation powers and instead establish a 100% gold and silver redeemable currency. At the very least, we should repeal the restrictive legal tender laws that force people to accept the government's fiat paper money, and set up a rival gold coin standard that is impossible for the politicians and bankers to debase.

A return to the gold standard would serve to reign in excessive fiscal spending and curb the accumulation of a massive (and increasing) national debt. By linking the Rupee to gold, Pakistan's currency would be catapulted into one of the most valuable and sought after currencies in the world, enabling economic stability, prosperity and peace of mind for millions.

They say history repeats itself, and it is clear that the tide of history is already turning against us. The collapse of many previous nations was down to the depreciation of the monetary unit. Monetary inflation led to their downfall, and the same will happen to us. No matter how many lies and reassurances we may hear, no fiat paper money system ever lasts for long. Eventually, the value of the Rupee will dwindle into nothing. Lest we be deluged in the coming catastrophe, we must repent and reform - before it is too late.

6

ON INFRASTRUCTURE

"Their insatiable lust for power is only equalled by
their incurable impotence in exercising it."

Winston Churchill

Disintegrating roads; naked and exposed power lines;
constant load-shedding; shambolic railways; obsolete,
overburdened sewerage systems - just a few of the countless
dangers the Pakistani population is exposed to every day
through the gross incompetence of their government. How can
the present backwardness of public infrastructure be explained?
The answer is simple.

Infrastructure is a service under public ownership. The
blatant endangerment of people's lives is simply an automatic
by-product of socialistic State control. The government has long
seized control of the building, operation and maintenance of all
infrastructures - the true cost of its decisions is not clear, but
what is certain is that it has failed to create systems that are
anywhere near fit for purpose. The entire enterprise is a
shambles and seems almost specially designed to inflict
maximum inconvenience on the common man and despairing
taxpayer.

Often politicians and beaurocrats can seem remote and
faceless, but what must be understood is that they, (whether

held accountable or not), make life and death decisions every day. Whereas their successes will improve the quality of life of many, their failures can result in catastrophic losses to countless lives, limbs and properties. Yet although they hold the mantle of power, they seem unwilling to undertake the necessary steps that this nation so desperately needs.

But what of the voiceless innocents? What of the tens of thousands of poverty stricken people whose lives are brutally cut short by contaminated drinking water resulting from the criminal negligence of feckless authorities? And those killed because of the gross disrepair of the roads and public transport systems? What of the millions of very young and elderly who suffer because of the never-ending load-shedding that occurs repeatedly without warning or mercy? How many more innocents must become casualties before the Pakistani people wake up to the inconvenient truth?

The truth is this: they know the State authorities are responsible, but what they have not yet come to terms with is that these same authorities will never change. We have been waiting for decades, and at this rate we will be waiting for many more. They simply have no incentive to improve. The incentives that would motivate private firms to become more efficient, competitive and determined to deliver quality do not exist for government bureaucrats. Bureaucrats under socialistic States are not accountable to the people for their actions, and if accused, they will simply pass the buck, deny all responsibility and then have the gall to issue press releases that document their scanty achievements.

Clearly, they have failed, and we can no longer be satisfied with the status-quo. The stakes are just too high. The importance of establishing, sustaining and continually improving the infrastructure that allows an economy to function properly is too critical a task for it to be jeopardised by incompetence. In order to maximise the chances that the quality and quantity of national infrastructure will be able to keep pace with a burgeoning economy and not encumber its growth, it is essential to take infrastructural decisions out of the hands of these underachievers. The fact is, the State cannot compete with the private sector when it comes to its sheer ability to get the job well done. Once again, it is to the private sector we must look for motivation, innovation, flexibility and efficiency.

People generally tend to assume that anything that is used by the public can only be publicly owned. Further, it is assumed that the vast swathes of publicly owned infrastructure such as roads, railways and communications networks could never be privately owned and operated. Socialist politicians and their minions like to encourage this premise and have been so successful in recent times that a question to the contrary is rarely posed. The public ownership of infrastructure built and operated by government authorities on behalf of the public has almost become a fundamental axiom. Yet, there are countless public spaces that are actually privately owned: pleasure gardens, restaurants, shopping malls, theme parks and cinemas to mention just a few. Clearly they are not of a substandard quality because they are not publicly owned - quite the contrary.

Let us turn to the road system. Poor quality roads are a common feature in developing countries (or at least those not blessed with copious oil). Good roads are the exception rather than the rule. The problem cannot be a lack of funds as the government always seems to have a perpetual supply of money ready to be frittered away. Rather, the problem lies in the way that government bureaucrats have assumed control and responsibility over the building and maintenance of roads while being incapable of discharging that responsibility. It is purely and simply a problem of incentives. Without the incentive for road builders and operators to compete with rivals on quality and price, the result will always be a road system that is inefficient and prone to breakdown. Just look to the predictably gridlocked traffic on the main roads of our inner cities during certain times of the day and the havoc that results.

But why does this happen? To answer, let us ponder over the bafflement we often feel when reminded of the crippling shortages of goods and the long queues in the few communist nations that remain. We may feel smug in the knowledge that our relatively freer economy is superior as our supermarket shelves are stacked high and deep. We understand that if the government deliberately sets the price for goods or services below the market rate, demand will rise but of course, producers will stop producing. Why then, can we not see that a traffic jam is one and the same thing?

Think of a road as a service being offered to motorists to get their vehicles from point A to Z. What is a traffic jam if not a queue for the use of the road caused by excess demand and insufficient supply? Is it not because the government has set the price of using the road at below the natural free market rate? Roads are paid for indirectly but they are free to access by anyone at any time, thus the effective price to use them at the 'point of use' is zero rupees. Obviously this is below the market rate, and as economic law dictates, if the price of a service is free, the demand for it will be infinite. Everyone and anyone will wish to make use of the road and this will cause congestion. If the price mechanism, the natural process that automatically brings equilibrium and stability to the market is removed, then the ensuing breakdown of the system is inevitable.

The illiteracy in basic economic principles of the vast majority of the population is perhaps not a surprise, nor is it too great a problem. But to expect the same from supposedly educated and worldly wise leaders and graduates from the better Western universities is a crying shame. Dwight Eisenhower's quip may explain the predicament: *"Farming looks mighty easy when your plough is a pencil, and you're a thousand miles from the corn field."* Let's face facts. If it is impossible to control the market for a simple fruit like apples without causing shortages or wasteful excesses, then how can it be possible to control the complex transport network of a sprawling, growing metropolis?

All people want is to simply acquire what they want easily and without fuss. But they are often foiled because knowingly or unknowingly, beaurocrats in ivory towers throw spanners in the works. No surprise here. They can hardly be expected to manage a distant system with countless variables. When their decisions go wrong, and they often do, they can only resort to their default mode of 'damage limitation'. But their responses are too crude and too slow. In the meantime, people may die, and countless hours and rupees are forever lost to Pakistan's economy.

The 'urban crisis' is a common term nowadays that is used to describe the blatant anarchy in our modern inner cities. Traffic jams, congestion, excessive pollution and chaotic public transport are only a few examples of the work of well meaning government authorities. Worst still, the crisis threatens to hinder the rapid economic growth that Pakistan so badly needs. This cannot be allowed to happen. A nation's infrastructure is equivalent to the veins and arteries of the human body. Any weaknesses, blockages or bottle-necks can cause untold damage elsewhere.

Due to the immense inter-relations and inter-dependencies that exist in the economy, such problems will cause other activities to become distorted. If unchecked, they may even spread to an eventual collapse. It is clear to see that this is happening in our towns and cities as we speak. The urban crisis does not act on a local level but interferes with the effective day-to-day operations of businesses and households everywhere. When the economy is not given enough slack because its infrastructure is inadequate, then only disorder can result.

Perhaps one of the most infuriating features of the urban crisis is that even when government authorities take the initiative to solve problems that they have themselves created, they do it in complete disregard to the welfare and convenience of the community. Take the common example of road repairs. Maintenance crews will arrive on a scene, section off a piece of road and dig it up at their own convenience. The work may take hours, weeks or even months. Yet no apparent thought is given to the inconvenience being imposed on thousands of travellers. As soon as roads are laid and resurfaced (often poorly, and with the most deplorable quality materials), they are dug up again to lay water, cable and gas lines, causing repeated aggravation to the public and interfering with personal and commercial business.

It is not even uncommon to see a piece of road that has been sectioned off to travellers but has no working crew. The traffic may be backed up for miles but the authorities have no concern about actually getting the work done as quickly as possible in order to reduce the inconvenience to the public. Indeed, the thought could not be further from their minds. One wonders if the government has ever taken the trouble to calculate, even estimate, the cost to business due to the delays resulting from this horseplay. The total cost to industry and personal households is difficult to quantify, yet few doubt that it must be incalculable in terms of money, time and frustration. Wasted fuel costs alone will be staggering. Through every stage, the road planning authorities have scant regard for the convenience of the public.

Take the rail network for example: it is in the grip of a State monopoly. It has had no chance or incentive to improve for decades and has predictably turned into an outdated mess. Railway crossings in urban centres look more like warzones. It is as if the government cares little for the safety of the public. Tragically, passengers are too often victims of appalling safety standards and the horrific train crashes that result. Stations, tracks, and trains are in a state of disrepair. Punctuality rates are poor, yet government authorities have no real incentive to improve the quality of services or offer value for money for passengers.

But why would they? State monopolies always remain immune to the dynamic pressures of a competitive environment. Changing management structures or injecting more funding will not help. Only a vigorous competitive market for rail travel can improve the experience of passengers. The only solution is to break up this artificial monopoly and privatise its constituent parts as soon as possible. Only this will bring about the better quality services that the populace expects and deserves. In the meantime, it is a credit to the travelling public that they are able and willing to tolerate these adverse conditions so patiently.

There are so many issues to be resolved that the mind reels. Roads are of a substandard quality and the ever disintegrating railways are congested, unpleasant and dangerous. Sewerage, drainage and sanitation barely exist at all in many areas and even minor rain results in floods that ruin land and property. Water quality lacks consistency at best; and at worst it spreads contagion through harmful water-borne bacteria and viruses and threatens health and even life itself. Through impure and unreliable water supplies, disease often spreads like wild fire. Landline communications networks are meagre, and lines are of a highly inconsistent quality. Again, these are State monopolies at work.

Considering that Pakistan is a declared nuclear power, the energy shortage is a source of acute shame and embarrassment. Flagrant wastage, inefficiencies and systemic failures by the State authorities responsible for these matters mean that energy supplies are sporadic and power cuts can sometimes last for days. In the extreme weather conditions of summer and winter, power cuts are tortuous to endure and a few vulnerable elderly and young simply do not survive them. These are just a few of the many wonders that dog-like subservience to Western socialism has created in our country.

We must break up these obscene State monopolies and privatise vast swathes of the public infrastructure. Some may ask if this is even possible. Others may ask how we can be certain that if the public infrastructure were under the control of the private sector whether things would even improve. The answer to that question is deceptively simple... incentives. Under the private sector, businesses and organisations would have an incentive to improve the quality of infrastructure and would be highly unlikely to be content with sitting on their hands as beaurocrats do now.

* * * * *

There are many types of infrastructural systems, but for ease of understanding, let us select just one for a more detailed look. Let us take the example of road infrastructure. If a private profit maximising business came into possession of a road, how would things change? For one thing, this would be a commercial organisation whose purpose is to make money for its owners, shareholders and stakeholders. The company would quickly address maximising sales while reducing costs and especially waste. The road owner would probably and quickly impose a toll. This would provide a constant, regular income along with clear usage statistics to assist with planning, services and financial control.

The technology that enables this is commonly used around the world. Automatic Number Plate Recognition (ANPR) is able to recognise unique registration numbers as vehicles pass. Alternatively, in-car sensors which provide a unique vehicle signature can be fitted to every vehicle cheaply. Tolls can be collected via toll booths or by periodically billing or debiting accounts. Toll booths and plazas are probably the easiest option and the quickest to commission.

The road owning business would then attempt to encourage as many people as possible to use its road by making the journey along it as convenient, quick, safe and pleasant as possible. On rural routes it is possible that a road owner would, to an extent, enjoy a captive audience but urban road networks in modern towns are complex webs that comprise a myriad of main roads, side roads and underpasses. There are innumerable ways to get from point A to point Z and no one road is likely to enjoy a monopoly. Therefore roads will all be competing with each other for vehicles or 'customers'.

As we know, competition between goods and services, when allowed to be conducted freely and without external interference, results in higher quality and lower costs. Rival firms would thus compete away 'abnormal' profits to 'normal' profits that would allow them to just about cover their costs and make it worth their while. The price of using the roads would thus be minimal to the average user, and far less than is currently charged indirectly through taxation.

Unlike the state of roads managed by the government, private road owners will understand the fundamental necessity of maintaining roads to at least minimum standards. After all, in order to ensure the loyalty of its customers, standards must be kept uniformly high. They will have a sharp incentive to repair a road that has suffered damage as soon as possible. It is anathema to lose revenue to rivals (this includes advertising revenue from roadside hoardings). Road works will hardly ever be seen during the day let alone rush hours. Road owners will have a huge incentive to conduct repairs at night which will be their least profitable time and to bring any such repairs to a swift conclusion. Of course the greater the delay, the greater would be the losses in revenue. When it comes to road maintenance for government authorities it is a question of their benevolence. With private firms, it is a matter of commercial necessity. The difference is quite profound.

Currently, if the poor quality of a road results in injury to pedestrians or damage to vehicles (as it often does), then there is absolutely no possibility of the injured parties sighting negligence, and acquiring compensation from the road owner, namely the government. The authorities of course claim to be working in the interests of the public. Yet they will do everything and anything to protect themselves when subject to real accountability. They will even enact laws to do so. This would change completely when roads are freed from government clutches.

Injured parties would be able to file lawsuits against road owners and operators. Naturally, the owners will have taken insurance against such eventualities. The worse the state of the road, the higher the premium they would have to pay the insurance company - yet another incentive to invest in quality road materials and improve standards. Although roads would automatically be maintained to minimum standards through competitive pressures as mentioned earlier, the vulnerability of road owners to civil or even criminal lawsuits would serve as a prudent backup.

Currently the situation requires that all vehicle owners pay a myriad of taxes and charges for the privilege of driving. All such revenues go into a 'road pot' which is ring-fenced for road building and maintenance at the discretion of bureaucrats. Save for petrol and CNG taxes, drivers are charged the same, regardless of their road habits. So the professional driver who may drive many hundreds of miles a week is charged the same as the elderly couple who go out just once a week for grocery shopping. This nonsensical and unfair approach leads to wastage and distortion. Drivers in this situation are not fully aware of the costs that they are imposing on society or on the environment when they travel.

The private solution to road ownership has a distinct sense of morality. People should be charged according to how much they use the roads. Of course, those who drive more cause more wear and tear so it seems entirely reasonable that they should contribute more. Why should the elderly couple who go shopping once a week pay for damage on the roads that they do not cause, and why should the professional driver pay less then the cost of the damage he causes? Also, heavier vehicles that by their very nature cause disproportionate damage should be charged accordingly. Costs should be made crystal clear and not diffused and hidden as they are now.

Thoughtless drivers who drive to the local store when it's within walking distance might think twice before they turn the ignition. Through private jurisdiction, congestion and traffic jams would become a mere footnote of history. Under free markets, the true price of travel would reach equilibrium where demand equates with supply. During rush hours, it is very likely that the price of using certain roads would increase slightly. Drivers would make a conscious choice, *"Is it worth taking my car today?"* Those travellers whose journeys are not crucial enough for them to be willing to pay a few extra rupees are likely not to make the journey at all. Just as there are no shortages of goods at private supermarkets because the price mechanism is allowed to function freely, there would be no shortage of road space, or 'queues' for roads. In this way, congestion would be eased and perhaps even eradicated.

The public transport system would receive a boost. Buses would not be marginalised in the new system. True the average car passenger is likely to be wealthier than the average bus passenger, yet the fact that forty of the latter are in the same vehicle and taking up not much more road space would enable them to receive very favourable treatment from the road owner. Buses would effectively be able to 'out-bid' other road users for use of the road. As such, public road transport would flourish.

It is even likely that the needs of public transport would be given priority in the design of new private roads. These new roads, bridges and underpasses springing up according to demand, would be financed by entrepreneurs and designed and built with the aim of maximising the flow of traffic. Making travel as convenient as technologically possible for motorists would be the aim of these improvements. The result would be a mass transit system that would run far better.

Under a private system, motorists would be more aware of the true costs that they impose on society when it comes to pollution. With road owners being corporate entities, they would be accountable to those environmentally affected by their operations. With traffic being a cause for pollution on roads, and this pollution lowering the quality of life in surrounding areas, under a sound justice system, road owners would have to pay their dues to society.

With surrounding businesses and residents given credence to complain and take steps through courts when their property rights are thus violated, the costs of pollution would be passed directly to the cause - vehicle owners. High polluting vehicles would thus be charged higher costs and a flexible price plan would emerge. Current technology already makes this possible. Higher costs would not be imposed across the board but specifically to the relatively higher polluters. This would no doubt also encourage the use of more environmentally friendly vehicles over time.

It is a certainty that roads would become safer for all users. Road owners would seek to insure their property, just like any other business. As is patently obvious in Pakistan today, the authorities have no incentive to enforce road safety standards, so they don't even bother. But private road operators would find it 'more profitable' to reduce accident rates and would attempt to manage the flow of traffic carefully to this effect. Pedestrian crossings would appear at opportune places and it is very likely that footpaths would be built to separate pedestrians from vehicle traffic. In residential areas, the building of footpaths may even become mandatory in the minds of developers. Road owners would respond naturally to the needs and wants of their customers as all homeowners would pay charges to their local road owners instead of paying local government taxes.

With the ability to keep track of all vehicles, road owners would financially penalise irresponsible vehicle owners who have inadequate or no insurance by charging in proportion to the risk that they incur on others. On our roads today, manic driving is the norm. It is a veritable free-for-all, with virtually no courtesies or mercies ever extended to other road users. Drivers are not financially accountable for their bad behaviour because the roads are 'public'. But under a private system, driving uninsured and in an irresponsible manner would soon dissipate as road owners would pursue bad drivers for endangering their business operations through the courts in an effort to extract compensation. The government on the other hand, seems incapable of ensuring that all vehicles and rivers on the roads conform to minimum safety standards unless through unenforceable laws and decrees.

We have looked at the road system in particular, but through these same principles of entrepreneurial incentives, the railways could be revolutionised, communications networks could be revamped, and sanitation and sewerage systems could actually be made to work. Energy and water supplies would become consistent and efficient, and precious lives would not be lost needlessly. The incompetent and incoherent policies of government would cease. Users who now pay the same levels of tax regardless of their individual needs would become consumers, paying only for what they use. Thus the wealthy and powerful who over-indulge in their consumption of the nations scarce resources would pay their way and would no longer be subsidised by the harassed middle class tax payer as is currently the case.

This is the only way forward. It is the only way the operators and owners of infrastructure can become accountable to their customers and environmental costs can finally be factored into total costs, incentivising everyone to pollute less and leaving us with cleaner, greener towns and cities. Businesses and organisations would be able to flourish in an environment where all costs are true, everyone pays their dues and expects the same from everyone else. No leaching off others, no free rides - a true win-win scenario.

The political challenges in implementing this system are immense. But for the welfare of the people and the rapid economic development of the country, it is absolutely imperative that they be overcome. There are countless interest groups that would resist such revolutionary changes. Selfishly, they would only seek to protect their own pockets. But what must be understood is that if these changes are not brought into being, the consequences will be even bleaker than current trends project.

Although free markets are not perfect, they are vastly superior to the current unworkable model. Just take a look around. The private sector already outperforms beaurocrats in almost every single respect, and business is the only economic mechanism in Pakistan of genuine innovation and progress. We can no longer endure a situation where inadequate infrastructure holds back Pakistan's ascent.

Make no mistake, infrastructure is vital - just look at how it is preventing the supposed rise of our eastern neighbour to 'superpower' status. But likewise, as our own economy grows it will place greater demands on our infrastructure which our authorities are incapable of fulfilling. In 1877, Lord Salisbury noted that *"the commonest error in politics is sticking to the carcass of dead policies."* Let us take heed and not continue to cling to policies and institutions that are relics of another era.

8

ON EMPLOYMENT

"In splendour, in seduction and in grace,
Their Banks out-soar the Houses of God.
In appearance trade, in reality gambling,
Profit for one, for thousands sudden death,
Science, philosophy, college, constitutions,
Preach man's equality and suck men's blood.
Want and idleness, lewdness and intoxication,
Are these the mean triumphs of the Occident?"

Allama Iqbal

Since time immemorial, we have used our resourcefulness to invent tools and instruments that save our manual labours and increase our rate of production. The concept of invention is an ancient one and in the modern age, we have more opportunity than ever for leisure because we have devised technologies that increase the efficiency of our exertions. We have managed to extend the boundaries of our expertise to address the needs of our day to day lives, adopting labour-saving devices into our homes which allow us to free time away from time-consuming chores. Thus we continue to develop a way of working that increases the accuracy of our production with a minimal input of effort.

This also applies to employed work. The occupations and vocations of old are soon overturned by the changes that new technologies bring to the modern world. But whatever the nature of work, age-old or modern, the need for people to earn a living wage remains a constant. Thus levels of overall employment are an important indicator of the health of an economy. Today, many commentators believe that the achievement of higher rates of employment should be given the highest priority in formulating economic policy. This is what we all wish: that no man be in want of a job or unemployed through no choice of his own. But if the highest possible level of employment is a desirable goal, then we must admit that our attempts thus far have been a failure. However, there is a way of achieving this objective, but it is only possible if we first illuminate ourselves to certain economic realities.

We must realise that employment is merely a means for producing valued goods and services. Employment is the means, and *production* is the end. It is *production* that matters most, because it is not the lack of employment, but rather the lack of sufficient *production* that causes scarcity and poverty. To illustrate the case, a country can enjoy 'full employment' (where every able bodied person is in work), and yet still be poor if the nature of most paid work is of the low-wage, low-productivity variety - such as the kind provided by near-subsistence agriculture.

Communist states achieve 'full employment' by force, and yet they still remain desperately poor. The Soviet Union achieved full employment for decades, and yet the average wage remained pitifully low and rampant poverty persisted. Why? It was because full employment was enforced through diktat. Kremlin beaurocrats could never have been successful in allocating workers to where they were needed most. Their flawed decisions resulted in tragic outcomes. Under that despicable regime, fellow 'comrades' were arbitrarily allocated according to what apparatchiks in Moscow thought was the best place for them to be.

While spewing propaganda about workers rights, the communists deliberately sacrificed workers pay and conditions on the altar of command and control despotism. They arbitrarily manipulated levels of production, and the sheer inefficiencies generated by such practices meant that they had to keep wages static. Faced with increased prices of material goods, food and fuel (due to central-bank instigated inflation), workers actually saw their wages decrease in real terms. History has demonstrated that consistently high levels of good quality, productive employment can never be achieved under interventionist socialist systems.

The lesson to be learned is that if the quality or level of production is ignored, then a government can artificially create an economy with full employment with relative ease. Indeed, by recruiting unemployed workers into the public sector and subsidising those in the private sector, full employment can quickly be achieved in any country. However, this is by no means useful, desirable or even moral. Many workers would be engaged in largely unproductive work, and this would have no material effect in increasing national prosperity and wealth. Thus it is not just employment, but the over-all *productivity* of employment that creates wealth and reduces poverty.

If instead of seeking to maximise employment we seek to maximise p*roduction*, we will find that all the 'inputs' in the economy (land, labour, entrepreneurship and capital) will be utilised in their most effective manner. However, prioritising production does not mean neglecting labour (employment). Labour is a primary 'input' and a critical part of the mix. If part of the labour force is involuntarily unemployed, 'maximum production' cannot occur because some of the input potential of the national economic equation remains idle and unused. Thus economic output will not be as high as it could be. Simply put, unemployed workers who are willing to work cannot find jobs, and in their idle state they cannot add to national production. Thus 'maximum production' can only occur if every worker is gainfully employed, so in effect, a natural and automatic consequence of 'maximum production' *is* 'full employment'.

Quaid-e-Azam himself emphasised the importance of production. His speech inaugurating the State Bank of Pakistan contains many pearls of his wisdom this nation has since forgotten: *"The monetary policy of the bank will have a direct bearing on our trade and commerce, both inside Pakistan as well as with the outside world and it is only to be desired that your policy should encourage maximum production and a free flow of trade."* Note that he specifically used the words 'maximum production.' In terms of economic policy, this was the most important speeches he ever gave, and the fact that it was his last also means he chose his words very carefully. Note also that he did not mention employment. He knew that if the government concentrated on maximising production, employment would take care of itself.

Possessing the prodigious work-ethic that he did, Quaid-e-Azam lived by the notion of the superiority of work over idleness - he is an example for us today. Work is important. A man out of work is unable to contribute to the betterment of his family and society at large. In that regard, the State has often tried to act to reduce unemployment levels in Pakistan. Many governments have made the attempt, but sadly, most of these proposals have been based on the entirely misinformed premise of increasing the number of jobs in the public sector. The reasoning is that this mops up the idle workforce and puts people in work. But there are inherent dangers. The greater the size and scope of the public sector, the more the bureaucrats needed to administer it. And as the public sector becomes ever more bloated and burdensome, the more inefficient and ineffective it becomes. All the while, costs spiral.

Some public sector jobs are essential and useful, but most public sector work consists of fluff that brings little value and plays no part in increasing national wealth. This 'make work' rather than 'do work' workforce would be far better utilised in the private sector. Here its expertise could be used more efficiently in creating the goods and services required by the nation. It is in the private sector where the majority of national wealth is created and sustained. So in general, there are two types of employment, *good* (private sector) and *bad* (public sector), and a government should do all it can to encourage the growth of the wealth-creating *good* kind while eradicating the wealth-consuming *bad* kind for which *it* is responsible.

The blame for why there are so many unemployed needing to be absorbed into the public sector in the first place ironically lies with the State itself. In a perfect world, willing workers would have many opportunities in the private sector, but the private sector simply cannot expand and utilise the idle unemployed because it is far too burdened by regulation, punitive taxation, and State corruption. Businesses can only expand in a productive fashion and employ more workers if the day to day decisions of managers and entrepreneurs are not needlessly distorted by government failures and crude interventions.

If only it were left alone, true free enterprise economics would be able to 'maximise production' by allocating the nations scarce resources of land, labour and capital most efficiently. Quaid-e-Azam called it *"free flowing trade."* Only this can lead to 'full employment', and not jobs consisting of poor quality work, but the best, most productive and useful jobs. It is simple to see why free enterprise systems lead to superior results. In free market nations, only goods and services for which there is a demand are produced. Non-interventionist governments recognize the futility of producing subsidized goods for which there is no market.

The decisions of ordinary households rule the day. As businesses become better at catering to household consumer demands and compete with each other to fulfil them, the productivity of their workers increases as they become more skilled. Successful businesses earn profits and thus increase wages in order to attract the most qualified workers when expanding. In order to create or maintain a competitive advantage over rivals, firms compete with each other not for the least expensive, but for the most *productive* workers. For a worker, higher productivity brings higher value, and firms will enthusiastically compete with each other to recruit the most valuable employees. This is the kind of system that offers sustainably high wages that continue to rise naturally.

This does not happen in just one business or industry, but throughout the entire economy. The cumulative effects of entrepreneurship, greater worker expertise, and the higher productivity gains that result from free enterprise work on a macro-scale. Increases in national production lead to increased per-capita incomes and this disproportionately benefits those who are poorest. As long as 'central bank instigated inflation' is eliminated, millions will be better able to afford essential necessities (food, shelter, basic clothing) that were earlier denied to them. Their conditions will be hugely uplifted, allowing them to be absorbed into the expanding middle classes.

As living standards rise, necessities and basic consumer goods become more affordable for the poor and have a profound change on their lifestyles and that of their families. They derive significantly higher satisfaction from their dramatically improved circumstances (from their personal viewpoint), than the rich who may merely buy yet more unnecessary luxuries that will not change their lives in as drastic a fashion. It works in simple ways. To give an example, automatic appliances such as washing machines and dishwaters make no difference to the wealthy - they have numerous servants. But to the working class housewife, they would make an enormous difference to her quality of life. The benefits of increased productivity, the availability of cheap consumer goods and increasing wages are therefore most enjoyed by the poorest.

* * * * *

A relatively simple concept but one that is rarely understood by the public and by policymakers alike is the effect of the forces that determine wages in a free market. Wages are simply the price of labour. Just like any other price, a wage cannot be arbitrarily 'fixed' without causing shortages and surpluses in the market for labour. Equilibrium can only be properly determined by the forces of supply and demand. For example, let us examine the market for a crop such as wheat and the effects of possible price controls.

If the government artificially raises the price of wheat to appease the farming constituency, farmers will be incentivised to produce more wheat because they can suddenly secure a higher price and possibly a greater profit in the market. Yet at the same time, because of the price increase, the demand for wheat by consumers will fall. This will lead to an inevitable surplus in the market which will create tremendous waste. Mountains of wheat will lie rotting. This is the simple upshot of State controlled 'price-fixing'.

The dire consequences for the wheat market are much the same for the market for labour if a similar 'price-fixing' policy is enacted there. If politicians attempt to appease the working public by attempting to raise the average price of labour (wage) by decree, i.e. enacting a minimum wage law, then an automatic consequence of this is that employers will be incentivised (against their will) to fire en-masse their most marginal, lowest paid workers.

Why? Because by raising the price of labour for employers and making it illegal for anyone to be employed at below a certain wage, workers who are not productive enough to be worth this minimum wage will be priced out of the market for labour entirely. Effectively, a minimum wage policy will create an excess supply of workers in the labour market with fewer buyers (employers) for their services. The inevitable result - greater unemployment. Unless these marginal workers have the means and opportunity to retrain and learn skills in order to improve their productivity, they will become permanently unemployed for as long as the minimum wage legislation is enforced.

This is an axiom of economics. A minimum wage law is a direct cause of increased unemployment. Although the sentiment of aiding workers interests is laudable, the idea of imposing a minimum wage is totally counterproductive to the interests of the most vulnerable workers. Underpinning this is the foolish notion that businesses will not voluntary raise wages for workers unless they are coerced. This is simply not the case. In fact, wage rates are directly linked to productivity. History shows that as productivity rises, wages invariably follow close behind. Workers in advanced economies today enjoy relatively high wages, but these wages were not increased periodically by government decree or by union pressure. They increased naturally and organically as a result of the better use of technology, education and training, and the increased productivity that resulted.

Why is productivity such a critical factor in wage rates? If a worker is paid 1000 rupees a week, his employer will expect him to generate at least 1000 rupees in revenue in an average week. Any less, and the worker would be imposing a net cost to the business. Common sense suggests that a business cannot be reasonably expected to employ workers at a loss for very long. Thus if a worker's productivity is not enough to justify the minimum wage, he will be fired through no fault of his own. Unfortunately for him, he is on the wrong end of the sliding scale.

On this scale, the higher the productivity of workers, the higher the wages they will tend to be paid. This is why students toil for years to obtain qualifications and certificates. These credentials indicate to potential employers how useful and 'productive' a job applicant might be. The more a worker makes for his employer, the more his employer will be willing to raise his wages to retain his services rather than risk losing him to a rival. These wage increases continue while there is still a net benefit to the employer.

Employers compete against each other in employing the best workers and they do this by bidding up wages until there is no further marginal benefit in hiring more. This is why average wages tend to rise in line with production in a healthy free enterprise economy and it is why workers in advanced economies, where production is high, enjoy higher wages.

But not all workers are so productive. They may lack skills, experience - any number of reasons. Yet when a business is faced with a minimum wage law, it will never employ a worker whose contribution to the operation of the business does not equal or exceed this decreed minimum wage. Thus when a government imposes a minimum wage law it effectively condemns to permanent unemployment all those marginal workers who are not capable of earning that minimum. We are talking about the least skilled and most vulnerable people in our society who have already been failed by the State education system. It is an utter travesty that such a law can still exist in a supposedly sophisticated and compassionate society.

These laws are brought in with wide popular appeal and cynically brought to the statute books by politicians who should know better. We can only assume that either they are too cynical to care, or that they fail to understand the devastating effects of such policies on the poorest and most dispossessed in society. Thankfully, minimum wage laws, although addressed in the statute books, are rarely enforced in Pakistan, providing a rare case where the government's ineptitude in administering and enforcing the law has actually benefited the country.

If the law was actually widely enforced, millions would be worse than unemployed - they would be unemployable. This is not a compassionate policy. It deprives a man of the right to earn an honest living for his family that his cumulative abilities and skills would otherwise permit him to earn. Not only that, but wider society is now deprived of the services that he was capable of offering and willing to render no matter how modest those services were. We cannot make a man worth more by waving a magic wand, no more than a law can make him worth more by making it illegal for anyone to pay him less.

The only way to increase employment prospects for prospective workers is to increase their potential productivity through good education and training, and allow businesses to flourish though the vigorous expansion of free enterprise. It is the responsibility of the government to provide for those who cannot provide for themselves, but ratifying vain and cynical legislation is no substitute for real action.

Saint Augustine said, *"Pray as though everything depended on God. Work as though everything depended on you."* Truer words were never said. Yet too many of our compatriots are condemned to the misery of joblessness. The only way to rectify this is to pursue policies with an emphasis on *production*. This will bring profound social benefits. Increased productivity, higher wages and living standards allow for the eventual reduction of the time that needs to be dedicated towards work in order for people to survive financially. This leads to more opportunity for family time and leisure.

Contrary to Marxist fantasies, modernisation and industry does not lead to slave-like toil for more and more workers. On the contrary, technology allows workers to work smart instead of hard. As a nation increases its level of production and output, it has less need for as many people to be employed. It is not a coincidence that modern economies have eliminated child labour and the elderly tend to retire early. When Pakistan finally pursues wise policies and becomes increasingly productive as a nation, living standards will rise as the cost of living falls.

Compare this to now. Today the cost of living is constantly rising due to central-bank instigated inflation, and more and more women are being forced through economic compulsion to enter the workforce to support their families. But for our mothers, sisters and daughters, work should be down to free choice and not coercion. The social ills that these financial pressures lead to and the affect on our families and children are clear for all to see.

Our policymakers must maximise incentives to increase productivity but they must realise that this is only possible though true free enterprise. It is the only way to eliminate poverty and to reduce its shadow over the national landscape. Poverty results within households where breadwinners cannot win enough bread to support their families. It is a solemn duty of care on the part of the government to ensure that all workers and households have the opportunity for employment by maximizing the vigour of the private sector and allowing the free market system to function properly. This must be done. Poverty and unemployment could be reduced to minor dimensions if only the government would enact the path of wisdom rather than expedience.

9

ON DEFENCE

"The atom bombs are piling up in the factories, the police are prowling through the cities, the lies are streaming from the loudspeakers, but the earth is still going round the sun."

George Orwell

In 1998, when Pakistan tested a nuclear device in response to India's earlier detonations, I was only 16, but I knew then that this was something quite special. The sense of pride felt by Muslims all over the world was palpable. We revelled in the open astonishment shown by Westerners that our country had managed to achieve such a technological feat when it seemed like a basket-case so much of the time. More profound though, were the sentiments expressed by Muslims of other nations. Our hearts swelled with joy when we heard that for many, it wasn't just a Pakistani bomb, but theirs too. It was only years later that I realised that none had celebrated in the potential destructive power of the device, but in what it embodied. To an Ummah that had for so long been at the mercy of imperialism, aggression, and subjugation, for the first time in hundreds of years, a Muslim nation had achieved what had been lacking for so long - deterrence.

It was in the days and weeks following that we heard awe-inspiring phrases in description of our country: the arsenal, the sword, the fortress of Islam. At the time they were probably easily dismissed by most cynics, but they contained truth. Extraordinary odds were surmounted to develop these weapons. For a country like Pakistan that is seemingly lacking in almost all the trappings a nuclear power would normally possess, the achievement is almost supernatural. For certain, the triumph is a God-given gift. It was no coincidence that this crown was placed on the head of our nation. The bomb was surely indicative of Pakistan's manifest destiny for the leadership and protection of the Islamic world.

As Muslims around the world become victim to the ever more elaborate and cruel designs of the Western powers, Pakistan has demonstrated itself to be one of the few nations pressing on hard in building its military strength. But even though the nation is now equipped with sophisticated nuclear weapons, it still faces profound pressures. Indeed, because of the possession of this capability, many elements around the world who would have paid our country no heed now consider us a potential threat and are actively working against us. Whether in India, Israel or America, neocon Zionists and Likudniks are simply unable to stomach the existence of a Muslim nation in possession of nuclear weapons. Their black propaganda against Pakistan and their covert attempts to neutralise our nuclear arsenal have not gone unnoticed and must not go unanswered.

It is important to stay the course. Regardless of present troubles, Pakistan holds a unique position in the Ummah. It has a huge, devout, Muslim population; a professional and capable armed force; and nuclear missiles that can reach thousands of miles in every direction. Unlike other secular Muslim States, the Pakistani Republic was established on the foundation of Islam and combines this with religious freedom for all minority religions. Placed at one of the most important frontiers of the Islamic World, it must face down challenges from its hyper-aggressive neighbour which sees Pakistan as a major obstacle to its vain plans for regional hegemony. As a result of the constant threat from an enemy that is many times its size and power, Pakistan has been compelled to develop and maintain an army, navy and air force fully capable of deterrence. This is not a task for the faint of heart.

Over its turbulent history, Pakistan and India have fought many wars and skirmishes. In spite of the massive imbalance of power, Pakistan has fought all to stalemate and has only decisively failed once - the 1971 conflict. Here India took advantage of strife in East Pakistan (now Bangladesh) and sparked a separatist guerrilla movement. After inciting rebellion, the Indian army illegally invaded international borders and broke the nation apart. This was not an isolated incident. Since partition, India has rarely been shy in imposing its will on its neighbours. Even today, every nation in the region has a fractious relationship with the giant.

In recent years it has become increasingly clear that India, in spite of its liberal and open facade, contains fascistic Hindu Zionist elements that are simply unable to accept the existence of a strong and independent Pakistan. Their power and influence in Indian political and military circles is growing, and they are becoming ever more belligerent. This is evidenced by the fact that although India is itself plagued by many dozens of violent separatist movements, it continues to covertly sponsor ethnic separatism in Pakistan. Ludicrous ideas are thus being floated in traitorous circles of a breakaway 'Pashtunistan' and 'Sindhudesh'. These sinister campaigns to demoralise the Pakistani people and break the country up into bite-size chunks are being financed and supported by Indian intelligence agencies among others. This chicanery must be taken seriously and decisively countered.

Yet while our enemies seek the denuclearisation, disarmament and ultimately the dismemberment of our beloved country, our politicians have pursued a foreign policy that simply does not reflect this dangerous reality. Over the last few decades this foreign policy record has been rooted more in short term expediency than wisdom. Kneejerk blunders have often trumped a considered, well-thought out attitude to foreign nations that maximises benefits to Pakistan and the Ummah at large.

Being a regional power in a strategic location, Pakistan has interests in the region that will not change or diminish over time. All the more reason for a foreign policy to be devised and implemented that reflects this. Yet at enormous cost, our leaders have continually sold out the national interest for US dollars and assistance, believing that Pakistan is simply incapable of handling its affairs without resorting to a begging bowl. This shameful attitude sells our country short and makes a mockery of the hard fought, hard won independence that so many brave souls fought and sacrificed their lives for.

Pakistan is not a nation that should be badgered and bullied. We have an enterprising, diligent and courageous population of 170 million and we are not a minnow to be chewed up and spat out by others at will. As our Founding Father Quaid-e-Azam said, *"Our object should be peace within, and peace without. We want to live peacefully and maintain cordial friendly relations with our immediate neighbours and with the world at large."* Note that he did not mention a master-slave bond but a dignified relationship between equals. Yet our leaders still believe that this nation cannot survive without handouts. True enough, the economy is weak, and the nation's finances are often in a shambles, but we know that this can be very rapidly corrected by adopting smarter economic policies, many of which have been discussed in this text at length.

The relationship with America is a particularly thorny problem. Whereas our deep relationship with China is worthy and mutually respectful, the United States has a history of needlessly intervening in other nations affairs: preaching one policy while practicing another. At the time of writing, the US military has blundered into several countries in the region, inflaming tensions and provoking terrorism against the Pakistani State as a result of our government's seemingly unconditional support for US policy. Unfortunately for us, Pakistan is now seen as a collaborator in the occupation of Afghanistan. As such, the American alliance has come at an unacceptably high cost of innocent dead Pakistani civilians caught up in the resulting melee. President Ayub Khan was clearly not joking when he said, *"Being the enemy of the US is dangerous; being their friend is fatal."*

American military action on sovereign Pakistani soil has meant that otherwise peaceful provincial regions have been radicalised and deviant 'takfiri' insurgencies aggravated. The best way to calm tensions in both Pakistan and the wider region would be to withdraw support for United States military operations. Not only would this quell the violence against the Pakistani State and people, but it would be much appreciated by the populace at large who are fed up with the spinelessness of government policies. A more pragmatic view is essential. We cannot afford to jump on a spurious American 'War on Terror' bandwagon if it destabilises the region and puts innocent civilian lives at risk. Our support for US policy has left us hanging on the edge of an abyss. Now that the Americans have opened Pandora's Box, we have become the victim of countless evils.

Our foreign policy must be re-aligned to our interests, not those of others – our domestic policies too. Pakistan's policing and criminal justice system is clearly not up to the task. As has been demonstrated in many places around the world, when there is no sense of safety and security for the people, when there is no sense of protection from terror at the hands of other citizens or the State, and when there is no sense of societal calm, the natural functioning of society grinds to a halt. We did not instigate this chaos, but we must resolve it. The fight was brought to our doorstep and we have no choice but to bring the perpetrators to justice. But incompetence on the part of State institutions does not help matters.

The right to personal safety and security is the most fundamental duty that the State must discharge. Yet, it is breathtaking that in Pakistan this most critical of government activities has been neglected and ignored in favour or other more spurious undertakings. The government intervenes precisely where it shouldn't, and yet during this emergency when its presence is essential, it is nowhere to be seen. It is a great tragedy that where the State should have applied its enterprise and concentration, it has failed. If terrorists can get away with their terror because policing is weak and the courts are inept, then the social fabric of society becomes endangered.

Enough is enough. More effective policing and counterterrorism efforts are essential. Disorder and terrorism cannot be tolerated, and the people's inalienable right to be protected from coercion and violence must be secured by State authorities. One way out is by reviving the purpose for which our nation was created. We must abolish the imported Western law that is so badly failing us and implement the Shariah immediately. We need a streamlined and efficient justice, policing and prison system that actually punishes terrorists and their collaborators rather than letting them off scot-free.

* * * * *

For Pakistan, its vulnerable strategic position, insecure borders, and troublesome insurgencies constitute a realistic and high threat level. As any nation grows more prosperous it becomes essential for it to protect its interests and citizenry from envious aggressors, but national defence cannot be effective without being underwritten by robust economic strength and resilience. The state of the economy is a national security issue in as far as the economy of a country dictates the level of military spending that can be sustained and the duration its military forces can hold out in the event of a war. High military spending as part of the national budget is not necessarily a reflection of a nation's devotion to militarism, but may often be something of an obligation.

Wealthy countries can maintain massive expenditures on their defence while devoting only a tiny fraction of their GDP to it. Poor countries that wish to match the same level of spending necessarily have to devote a larger percentage of their GDP to the task. This is because military spending only makes sense in *absolute* terms. Essential armaments like tanks, jets and submarines are expensive, and to maintain an adequate defence it is necessary to possess a minimum amount of this hardware.

Less than this amount and defences will be too easily overrun in the event of a war.

This is a minimum absolute cost that Pakistan must meet or exceed. Thus we cannot lower our *percentage spending* on defence if it means that our defence is compromised, especially if the enemies defence spending is leaping ahead. Pakistan is facing an existential threat to its existence, so a balance between 'guns and butter' is largely irrelevant. Nobody wants an arms race, but it is a burden we have to live with.

Regardless of seemingly pointless 'confidence building measures' and cultural exchanges with India, we cannot fool ourselves into believing that we live in a new era of peace. As Plato said, *"only the dead have seen the end of war."* At some point there will be conflict. It has been prophesied. Foretold by the Noble Prophet (peace be upon him), the coming *Ghazwa-e-Hind* is a reality that the Pakistani nation and military must prepare for - mentally and physically. High defence spending therefore is absolutely critical in ensuring at least the bare minimum level of military capability against aggression. In a tense and uncertain geopolitical environment, the armed forces must be given adequate resources to preserve the territorial integrity of the nation.

But the symbiotic relationship between national strategic security and economic development cannot be underestimated. Neither can be achieved without the existence of the other. Fighting a war while burdened with a weak economy is like fighting with two hands tied behind ones back. However, the thought that military defence is underwritten by economic vitality is not one that has yet occurred to our leaders. The danger has now become potentially catastrophic. For far too long national defence expenditures have risen above and beyond the capacity of the national exchequer to burden, and thus our weak socialistic economy has become a national security menace.

The spoilers in high office are destroying from within what our brave young soldiers are trying to protect from without. As economic strength and stability have been undermined by failing socialistic policies, the result is that although ongoing investments in men and materials have resulted in a deterrent defence capability, it is one that is stunted in its potency by its inability to sustain even short term military operations. This not only puts the nation in jeopardy, but also the lives of the courageous men and women in the three armed services who risk everything for Pakistan every single day.

Unfortunately, past actions of policymakers in Pakistan make transparent their view that economic development is in a wholly separate sphere to the nation's defences. Defence and strategic threat reviews wax-political about the need for economic development, but nothing transpires. Time for a reality check. Trying to punch above ones weight is not a common sense approach. Bravado can only take one so far and military history shows that barring ingenious tactics, if a country is lumbered with a lacklustre economy and the bullets start to fly, it will not punch above its weight for very long. Romantic patriotism does not win wars. We can only project power when we have power to project, and this cannot be achieved without robust economic growth.

In addition, national power is not simply a reflection of economic and military strength, but also of diplomatic muscle. Building on friendships, alliances and trading and cooperating with other nations on amicable terms is an essential part of fortifying oneself and ones allies against aggression. The Sino-Pakistani alliance is an excellent example of how a convergence of interests has been nurtured over decades into a special relationship that is rarely seen in global politics today. But other allies should also be sought and other diplomatic ties built too; especially in the Muslim world where Pakistan should step in to take its place as a leader, perhaps as the instigator and leading power behind a new NATO style Muslim bloc. We must remember though, it is economic power and wealth built on sound foundations that will earn us the *credibility* that is such a crucial factor in such endeavours.

A century ago, Allama Iqbal foresaw the creation of a global federated union of autonomous Muslim republics. As others regions such as Europe, Africa and Latin America band together to unite, why can the Muslim Ummah not do the same? Perhaps it just requires one nation to ignite the spark. Working for the creation of the *'Federation of Islamic States'* must become an important plank in Pakistan's foreign policy. At the very least, the formation of a grand military alliance would be an important first step that is long overdue.

Pakistan was born to leadership. This is our task. We must revive ourselves, find our courage, and mobilise. I am reminded of the profound words of Shakespeare in Julius Caesar, *"Why, man, he doth bestride the narrow world, like a Colossus, and we petty men walk under his huge legs and peep about to find ourselves dishonourable graves. Men at some time are masters of their fates: the fault, dear Brutus, is not in our stars, but in ourselves..."*

For now, our national defence aims are introverted, but as Pakistan grows and takes on the mantle of Muslim leadership, these national security aims must evolve. Let us not forget that as we speak, many seemingly helpless Muslim countries around the world are being encircled and devastated by the Western powers. Shamefully, no Muslim country has yet mustered the strength or resilience to even intend on protecting the interests of fellow Muslims in need of rescue. As crimes are being committed against our brethren, we can no longer just sit and throw blame from the sidelines - we must act decisively. For the sake of the Ummah, it is time for a defender to arise. Pakistan is well-placed - so let us begin.

10

ON HEALTHCARE

"And he said unto them, Ye will surely say unto me
this proverb, Physician, heal thyself."

The Bible, Luke 4:23

We would do well to challenge politicians thus. Ask them, when considering the crises faced by people on a daily basis, to imagine that the affected person is a close friend or member of family. What would be the most favourable government policy? What measures could be taken in the best interests of the affected friend? How could that friend be best assisted in their predicament and how could that assistance be extended to people in a similar situation? Too often, solutions are forcibly imposed, and the wishes of people are ignored. But why not furnish people with the choice and power to determine their own fate while incentivising them to do the right thing? Or is it really better for government to impose itself - however bad the results?

Placing humanity and compassion back into the formulation of policy is long overdue. It has too long been sidelined in the dispassionate machinery of government. Policies devised by wonks in provincial capital buildings may seem to work on paper but it seems they rarely work in practice. Assumptions are arbitrarily made about what is best for people without taking into account what people consider to be best for themselves. The results are plain to see. We all suffer at the hands of pitiable government services. For example, if a family member was in dire need of medical treatment, would any sensible, caring person wish to send the patient to a woefully inadequate government run hospital? I suspect they would do everything in their power to find an alternative.

Yet poverty ensures that this is exactly what happens for many. Meanwhile, one wonders if the ideological extremists who loudly advocate their socialistic system would ever dream of using these hospitals and clinics themselves. It is an appalling, elitist state of affairs that breeds mass discontent. The blame lies with those who advocate precisely the wrong prescription to the problem. In response to the troubles caused by government, they call for even more government control. But let us be clear. The government has awesome powers at its disposal; thankfully, sometimes the maximum damage it can do is to inconvenience us, but when it comes to the all important issue of people's health and well-being, lives are at stake. People live or die by the decisions of beaurocrats.

Currently in Pakistan, the state of government run healthcare remains appalling in its quality, consistency, and cost effectiveness, and particularly in the medical value it provides patients. Most government run hospitals and clinics are inadequate and simply unable to offer the level of clinical care that people need and deserve. There are major inefficiencies, poor morale amongst doctors, nurses and administrators, and a profound lack of innovation that should be the hallmark of any medical service for the public. This is no accident. These hospitals are directly State run, and their poor standards are in marked contrast to the quality and cost effective services that private institutions provide all across the country.

The problem with government is its inflexible attitude. Since the creation of Pakistan, the same tattered old socialist dogma has been taken as gospel. Hospitals have been built, resources have been allocated, doctors have been trained, and yet the result of this socialised healthcare model has been the same as that of all similar models across the world. It has failed in achieving the goals that it was originally conceived for. But this is no surprise. As the experiences of other nations illustrate, it is difficult to achieve the awesome task of providing good healthcare for a population. Difficult yes - not impossible. It can be done, but only if we dispense with ideological bias.

One thing is for sure, the problem cannot be solved by the current method being employed. Even throwing more money and resources at the problem will not help. Regardless of the amount of finance injected, the healthcare system is clearly incapable of achieving success. It is institutionally 'unfit for purpose'. Instead of incentivising medical staff and administrators to optimise the level of clinical provision, the current system actually distorts, resulting in conflicts of interest, failures and inefficiencies. Ultimately along with the wastage of public funds, it is the patients that suffer.

Part of the failure to diagnose the problem is due to the dissonance between the perceived *inputs* into the healthcare system and the *outputs* that result. Once resources have been allocated and deployed by a government, the inputs (money, resources and staff) are easy to determine, but outputs can be difficult to pin down. Healthcare is, by its very nature, a somewhat nebulous service which is more qualitative then quantitative. Numbers and statistics such as those on health indicators, the number of vaccinations administered and the number of doctors available, do not give a good enough indication about the actual quality of care that is being administered to patients. They don't provide a good enough indication of whether services are actually value for money.

This is apparent from the healthcare experiences of many developing countries around the world. There are many examples of countries that expend considerable resources on healthcare while achieving very little in terms of quality clinical care for their patients. At the same time, there are examples of governments that expend relatively little, and yet achieve much better results. Again, it is not a question of throwing increasing amounts of resources at the problem and expecting things to improve.

Of course, the more the expended resources, the better the provision is *likely* to get, but account must be taken of the efficacy of the resources thrown into the pot. Care must be taken to determine the best model for allocating these resources in order to achieve the best results. This is even more critical in the case of a poor developing economy such as Pakistan. We have scant resources and must therefore concentrate our efforts wisely. Rich advanced countries can perhaps afford to spend recklessly, but we cannot.

The ailment at the heart of our current healthcare system lies in one issue - incentives. These are the incentives that affect the day to day decisions of the agents in the system namely, patients, doctors, nurses, pharmaceutical companies, administrators and medical scientists. In order to devise a system that works, it is necessary to motivate and encourage people across the service chain to play their part. The patient also needs to be incentivised. The patient is too often ignored, but he or she should have the incentive to consume only as many health services as are adequate for them to maintain a good standard of health. Just like any service, there is an optimum amount that can be demanded by a consumer which will satisfy their needs. On the other hand, there is such a thing as excessive and wasteful consumption of healthcare.

Theoretically there is practically no limit to the amount of healthcare that an individual could consume even if there is nothing essentially wrong with them. A person could arguably have a check-up once a day, every day, and consume precious health resources in the process. The effect of this on other, more worthy patients needs little explanation. 'Over-consumption' is not a good thing, but is inevitable if a service is offered 'free of charge'. Granted, there are many cases where unfortunate individuals require constant care, but for the majority, healthcare should only be consumed when necessary.

Why doesn't an exclusively government run single-payer system work? Because if health resources are provided free of charge at the point of use, then the law of supply and demand tells us that demand will be near infinite. No surprise here, because if the price mechanism is dispensed with, the result will always lead to imbalance. This is not efficient or sustainable. If the price of the service is artificially set at zero, demand inflates while supply struggles to keep up. The inevitable result is shortages in the form of the sick waiting their turn in a queue.

The price mechanism (which allocates goods and services) cannot function if the price is artificially set at zero or if the real price is hidden under many layers of bureaucracy. In such systems, the State tries to act as a 'single-payer' or financial intermediary and pays for all treatment. But if the State is paying for everything, the patient will not mind what their treatment is costing in terms of resources, or the impact they are having on other people in the waiting line - people who may be more medically deserving.

Generally speaking, in a private hospital setting, a doctor will take great pains to make the patient feel comfortable and offer the best possible service. After all, he is competing with other doctors for the patient's custom. If he fails in satisfying his patients he will lose them along with his reputation and will not remain a viable practitioner for long. But in a government run hospital, doctors are simply not as accountable because their patients are receiving the service via the aegis of the State. Odd perhaps, but since government care providers are not as *financially accountable* to the patient as they would be if they were practising in a private hospital, underperforming is a sad symptom of the systemic disease. Patients deserve value for their tax money, but sometimes they will not receive it.

This is because the treasury will pay regardless of the level of service the doctor or nurse provides. A bad doctor (they do exist), will therefore practise longer in a government hospital because there he is not as accountable to his patients. Yet he would not enjoy a similar length of tenure in the private sector. Doubters might like to examine their nearest government financed hospital and observe the quality of care provided for the average patient. The doctors are largely well trained and well intentioned. Basic healthcare is free to all-comers. But services are poor, waiting times are long, care providers are often insensitive to patient needs, and patients themselves are largely dissatisfied.

This is by no means a slight on the hardworking and decent doctors and nurses who practise from such hospitals. Not by any means. It is merely a comment on the 'systemic', unavoidable failures of the State controlled, single-payer healthcare model. Even good practitioners cannot buck the system. Put simply, because of the beaurocracy and lack of direct financial accountability to the patient, the agents in the process: doctors, nurses, and administrators are simply not incentivised in the correct manner to do their jobs in a way that maximises clinical care at a reasonable cost.

Universal health provision is an excellent ideal and should be pursued, but it cannot work like this. There is little or no positive incentivisation, practically no innovation, poor clinical care, and no transparency of cost. Many observers, commentators and politicians recognise these failings but they see the solution as being the injection of yet more resources and funding. They insist that 'under-funding' is the root of the problem. Yet increasing the budget will only kick the problem can down the road. More resources will not change the fundamental lack of incentives that patients and doctors are guided by every day.

If proof is required, simply look to the socialised universal-care systems in the West. They may look very impressive on the surface, but delve deeper, and you will find serious and altogether unsustainable problems. Even in these advanced nations, service loses its efficiency and costs spiral out of control while the quality of care remains stagnant or decreases. Their example shows that when the government acts a monopoly provider of healthcare. There is an absence of competitive pressures and thus there is no incentive for hospitals to provide value-for-money services or improve on the quality of their clinical provision. In spite of the massive increases in funding year on year, there are little improvements to the quality of care. Frequent shortages, long waiting lists and rationed clinical care are symptoms of this unenlightened policy.

This is what is happening in Pakistan too. Yes, there are some State healthcare institutions that are respectable but these are few and far between and they still suffer from problems. Were it not for the presence of the burgeoning private healthcare industry, there would be little decent medical provision at all for those who can afford it. But what about those who cannot? They have to endure substandard care in 'free' hospitals. This outdated and discredited model of universal care is not the way forward for Pakistan. If even modern nations with excellent administrative practices cannot make this model work, then there is no hope that the shambolic government of Pakistan ever could. It is a complex problem, but there *is* an elegant solution.

* * * * *

If we are to devise an ideal healthcare service, it must have certain characteristics that easily identify it as being sustainable and positive for all involved. First, it is essential that the system is transparent in terms of costs. The problem we have now is that the government acts as a third party between the patient and the practitioner. This creates a financially unaccountable barrier between the two and both have little idea of what is being charged.

In this scenario, the patient will too often end up in a long queue, and the doctor will too often charge too much for doing too little. All the while, neither will have an incentive to provide value to the taxpayer. An ideal healthcare model should ensure that the price-mechanism is central and that the costs that are incurred are real and apparent to both the patient and the doctor. A sense of value and financial responsibility is fundamental to the best healthcare provision.

Second, the emphasis must be placed on patient care and removed from needless, wasteful, expensive red tape and administration. A huge problem with our current socialised systems is the burden of bureaucracy, and the notion that we should create unproductive jobs for the sake of creating jobs. A State operated healthcare system wastes a huge amount of its budget, not on patient care or even remuneration for care practitioners, but on administration. Multiple administrational layers only get in the way of better clinical care. They should be cut out as much as possible.

Finally, another important characteristic of an ideal system is one where we incentivise innovation and invention in medical treatments and provision. It is well known that the greatest number of medical advances come from countries where healthcare is market or customer driven. Here medical scientists and pharmaceutical companies compete with each other to create innovative treatments and usher in medical advances. It is patients who benefit from this innovation. This generally does not happen under socialised systems due to the high level of bureaucracy and the stranglehold of the State.

There is an ideal healthcare solution. It fulfils the above criteria and does not rely on crude State control. It enables the provision of optimal, personal clinical care for every single citizen, while preventing the haemorrhaging of funds from the sparse State treasury. This solution correctly aligns the all important incentives that affect people's decisions and levels of performance.

Quite simply, the best way to achieve cost transparency, medical innovation, lessen administration, and yet maximise patient care and satisfaction is to put choice in the hands of the patients themselves. We should allow competition and free markets to improve clinical care and lower costs in the healthcare system. This means that clinical care should be removed from government control and should be in private hands where even now in Pakistan, it is flourishing so well. But the key is that not just a few, but *every* citizen should have access to the private health system. After all, we must have universal care.

The government can achieve this in a very simple manner. Instead of interfering in the nitty-gritty of healthcare like building hospitals, employing doctors and nurses, and providing direct (but substandard) healthcare, it should provide every individual citizen with a *healthcare account*. This is an account much like a current account, opened on an individual basis on behalf of every single citizen. This account will be directly credited by the government on an annual basis with funds to be used only for healthcare purposes. If the government refrained from wasting money on other failed healthcare efforts, and concentrated all of its healthcare resources on furnishing these accounts, they would be very well stocked.

The total amount credited into each individual *healthcare account* would be the same, if not more, as the government's desired *per capita* expenditure on healthcare. The funds would be tax free and could be used by the individual on any medical treatment they wished as long as it conformed to certain criteria of legitimacy. The choice of how the money is utilised would lie solely in the hands of the account holder. The funds deposited by the government would increase year on year in line with economic growth. Any unused funds would roll over to the following year.

This would bring about a healthcare revolution. Private clinics would spring up automatically in every small town and village, knowing that there was a local population that could afford their services. With a healthy balance of money to use at their discretion, all citizens would exercise free choice about where to go for treatment. Aware of how much they had to spend, they would be incentivized to shop around for the best value for money. With the free market liberated and able work its magic, clinical care would improve significantly while competitive pressures would force prices downwards. Today, only the well-to-do can afford the excellent private hospitals and clinics that exist all over Pakistan. Just imagine if every single Pakistani had access to them. This is what the *healthcare accounts* would achieve.

Along with the routine medical care that the accounts would provide, citizens may choose for part of the fund to be set aside to purchase *medical insurance* for emergency illnesses and injuries which would otherwise be beyond the pockets of many. From where this insurance was purchased would be at the discretion of the individual. Purchasers with freedom of choice would shop around to find the policies best suited to the needs of their families. Because the policies would only cover relatively rare catastrophes and chronic illnesses, the premiums would be affordable by all. Routine treatments and medicines would be easily paid for by the remaining funds in the account.

This scheme allows patient choice and so brings patients and care providers into a direct relationship with each in the same way that any other product in the economy is managed in a free market. Healthy competition would invigorate patient care. Just as private hospitals and clinics have flourished in recent years in our country, a vibrant health insurance industry would quickly develop that would compete for customers. The poorest would have access to it and would benefit most, after all, it is the poor who are most likely to fall ill and require medical treatment. Poor diets, inappropriate housing, health neglect and overcrowding all ensure this remains the case.

A scheme of this nature would be less expensive and bureaucratic than the current malfunctioning system. As many similar schemes around the world have proved beyond doubt, it would certainly be more satisfactory to the participants. By utilizing the powerful engine of free enterprise, there would be massive improvements over the current two tier arrangement where the rich are satisfied and the poor are left to suffer substandard care.

With *healthcare accounts*, the poor would have access to medical treatment *on par* with that received by the wealthy, no longer the meagre standard that the government currently inflicts them with. Too many of our fellow compatriots are short-changed by the inadequacy of our current system. This cannot stand. High quality universal healthcare is certainly possible, if only we find the wherewithal to make it happen.

11

ON POPULATION

"Say: 'Come, I will rehearse what Allah has prohibited for you,' join not anything as equal with Him; be good to your parents; kill not your children for fear of poverty - we provide sustenance for you, and for them, and come not near to shameful deeds whether in open or secret; take not life, which Allah has made sacred, except by way of justice and law."

Surah Al-An'am Holy Qur'an (6:151)

The family unit is the cornerstone of human existence. It is a social unit that forms the foundation of society: the cohesive glue that enables the social order to function with minimal friction. It is all the more important because we live in a society with an enormously complex array of unwritten rules, etiquettes and norms, and some can be difficult to comprehend. The typical family environment acts as a secure and protected cocoon from which our children are able to absorb the initial basics of social interaction and knowledge. It is from this safe environment under the watchful eyes of caring parents and elders, that young people are able to make their first forays into a bewilderingly complex world.

Given this, we would probably expect the State to, at the very least, take a benign view in its treatment of the family unit and avoid any policy or enterprise that might potentially cause it harm. Common sense would assert that the State would accept that parents are by far the best placed to administer the lives of their children, to care for them, and to provide for their fundamental needs. Surely we can agree that children are a sacred trust for their parents and can be relied upon to care for them responsibly.

Not so. According to the credo of socialism, we would be wrong. For a socialist, the utopian ideal exists when the life of every member of society is regulated and controlled from 'cradle to grave'. Through their constant social engineering, the decisions of beaurocrats in ivory towers override the fundamental rights of parents and guardians to choose what is best for their families. Yet although the vision of a perfectly harmonious and egalitarian society is a noble idea, when it is enforced through the powerful instruments of the State, the outcome is dire for the welfare of the masses.

The reason for this failure lies in the fact that people are highly complex creatures and thus difficult to predict or control. It is our lack of easy satisfaction in our environment, our lives and our circumstances that shapes our fickle nature. Thomas Edison noted that *"discontent is the first necessity of progress,"* asserting that it is one of our greatest human flaws that drives our perennial struggle to survive in an uncertain world. Imbued by our Creator in our inner consciousness, is a near irresistible will and desire to overcome all circumstances and strive for our betterment in whatever form we perceive it - and we are not always rational in our pursuits.

As mentioned in the Holy Qur'an often, part in warning, part as rebuke, Allah states that the desires and ambitions of mankind are never-ending and can never be quelled. Our ambitions are such that however high we reach, we are never satisfied. Through our persistence and aspiration, we are capable of achieving the most glorious feats and yet equally capable of the most heinous crimes. Whatever we choose to do with our lives, the divine gift of freedom of choice complements our mystical tendency to aspire, strive, risk, sacrifice, and accomplish.

Whether the State is a help or a hindrance, in the fabric of our nation, people must hold the most esteemed place. And the more the better - the greater the population, the greater will be the number of workers, scientists, technologists and entrepreneurs, and the greater will be our economic potential. But the sine qua non is that *every* person be enabled the opportunity to better themselves. Each person lives their lives in the pursuit of material, spiritual and emotional betterment and their contribution to society comes in countless forms. All should be allowed to take advantage of the considerable benefits of living in a growing economy.

Yet what we see on a daily basis are the aspirations of our youth being trampled by the incompetence of the State. Our people are increasingly angry and frustrated at the continuous malfunctions and histrionics of politicians. This is not a minor indignation, but a seething rage of Pakistan's 'coping classes' - law-abiding, hard-working, tax-paying citizens, who over the decades have despaired as their country's sovereignty has been dissipated, its economy compromised, and its people disrespected by a succession of political pygmies.

And there is surely nothing as brazenly presumptuous on the part of recent governments as their attempt for years to control the *size* of the population. Here, the masses, especially the poor, are bombarded with 'educational' propaganda in an effort to convince them of the virtues of the small family. Often bankrolled by foreign institutions such as the World Health Organisation, we witness everywhere the unseemly imposition of family planning and a savvy drip-drip indoctrination that discourages new births.

Advocates claim that the cause of the national malaise is that selfish families persist in having too many children and there are not enough resources for everyone. Yet champions of the 'overpopulation' theory cannot bring any evidence to bear to prove that a high population density has anything to do with the persistence of poverty. A simple look at real world examples illustrates how fallacious the claim is.

A country like Argentina has a lower population density than the United States but a lower per capita income level too. Japan is significantly more densely populated than Pakistan, yet our income level is a small fraction of theirs. Sub-Saharan Africa has an even lower population density than ours, yet they are even poorer. Some poor countries have high population densities, some rich countries have low population densities, but there is no consistent relationship between wealth and population. Beginning with Thomas Malthus, and continuing with errant social engineers today, many desperate attempts have been made to salvage the 'overpopulation' thesis. But they have all failed.

Poverty has nothing to do with either overpopulation, scarcity of arable land or lack of natural resources. There are innumerable examples of very wealthy nations that have never had decent arable land or resources (Japan, South Korea, Switzerland), and many examples of nations that have abundant natural resources and arable land but still remain impoverished (India, Brazil, Kenya). When we see crowded slums on the outskirts of our great cities, we may insinuate the easy conclusion that 'overpopulation' is the *cause* of poverty. But the causality is of the contrary.

These people are not poor *because* they live in densely populated slums - they live in slums *because* they are poor. Their poverty means that they are unable to afford the costs of living in a bona fide urban living space, yet they settle in slums because they are unwilling to forego the benefits of residing in an urban area. Slums grow due to economic depressions and increasing poverty, and also because for their residents, living in them still carries benefits in terms of costs, jobs, and amenities over living rurally.

It is *economic stagnation* caused by excessive State interventionism that is the key factor in poverty. Despite the many decades of socialistic planning in Pakistan, the economic, cultural, spiritual and social results have been catastrophic. There have been countless 'poverty alleviation' schemes, yet none has succeeded in making even the slightest dent. The population has been expanding fast but there has been no corresponding expansion in economic activity. The size of the economic cake grows only too slowly, if it grows at all, in spite of the fact that there are significantly more people taking a share day by day.

Of course, we know by now that this is because State interventionism induces inefficiencies and thus retards economic growth. But instead of changing policies, cynical socialist planners have worked out that if they are unable to increase income per person by increasing the size of the economy, then they may deceive their way closer to their objective by curtailing the *size* of the population. Thus it is only too easy for the elite intelligentsia to point accusatory fingers at poor families and lay blame on them of having *"too many children"*.

It is only too easy to pass the buck of responsibility for the failings of our nation from those in authority to those who are powerless. This political sleight of hand is still being perpetrated. Precious resources that could be used more sensibly to uplift our nation are instead being used to needlessly interfere with the private workings of ordinary families. A colossal waste of time, and a sad example of the cynical trends in our political culture.

Some may scapegoat the people of Pakistan for our country's lack of progress, but the reality is that our leaders *policies* are preventing new entrants into society: the youth, from successfully engaging in national life. Rampant unemployment and an appalling lack of opportunity are fuelling disillusionment and strife on a massive scale. Millions of young roam the streets and while away their days because government bureaucracy demotivates, extinguishing any flames of potential entrepreneurship. The miniscule levels of national economic activity are simply unable to absorb their labour.

More still, the overcrowding in urban centres is not caused by the presence of too many people but by the singular lack of housing and other amenities, all of which are directly or indirectly mis-regulated by broken State bureaucracies. Overcrowding is essentially a problem which manifests itself through shortages and surpluses caused by disequilibrium in demand and supply. Shortages in housing are primarily due to the inability of the market to correctly allocate space due to

State-induced malfunctions. Government regulations, obtuse rental legislation, inconsistent taxation, politically corrupt bank lending, and the subsidisation of housing are the prime causes of these distortions and the chaos that results.

Successive generations of politicians and leaders have attempted to build the nation's infrastructure from the top down. Thick files and folders brimming with schematics now fill offices in public buildings. If these plans were accurate, you would think that the nation would by now have been transformed into an idyllic Japan. But the material results of these schemes are nowhere to be seen. The old canard is inevitably wheeled out regarding the 'unmanageable' density of the population. But the infrastructural disarray in our towns and cities is the result of State manipulations in housing, amenities, roads, sanitation, and land. Population size makes no difference.

Population growth is not a cause of our national problems. Not at all. It is merely the unlucky scapegoat onto which blame is conveniently heaped in an attempt to distract the masses from the true cause of their lack of advancement. Government spin doctors have been uttering the same platitudes and banalities for decades, yet the impact of State policies has not even slightly matched their claims. The sole purpose of a government is to serve its people by enacting prudent and sensible policies in their interest. This cannot mean they can control their numbers in order to make life easier for themselves. Our leaders are continuing to cling to unworkable policies: policies which are the true cause of national lethargy, stagnation and strife, and they must change their ways.

Family planning is forced on the poor because the government does not believe that they can be trusted to correctly decide on how many children to have. Even the middle classes and elite are inclined to agree with the government line. In fact, this orthodoxy is rarely questioned. But do they consider why poverty stricken parents might want to have as many children as possible? The reason lies in the fundamental insecurities of poor parents, and more specifically parents who are struggling to survive and feed themselves.

Most people are level-headed, regardless of their illiteracy or lack of schooling. For those facing a daily struggle for food, clothing and shelter, simple economics is the priority. It transcends all other things: relationships, culture, sometimes even faith. Under these circumstances, when a man has no education, no worthwhile skills and no prospects, the wisest decision he can make is to marry and have as many children as possible. Children are valuable as income earners. Even at a young age they can contribute to the family table. The more the better. After all, there is the possibility that at least one child may find commercial success and provide the means to look after his parents in their old age.

What about the children's education? Well, even parents who have no education themselves and little worldly exposure realise that education is an investment for the future. Nevertheless, schooling is a cost to families even if the education is free. After all, children could be earning if they were not at school. Whether this sacrifice is worthwhile or not is determined by the quality of education and the likelihood of it resulting in employment.

But what have been the results of 'free' State driven mass education programs? Thousands of schools have been constructed, tens of thousands of teachers recruited, millions of children enrolled - but to what effect? Mass education aimed at the most disadvantaged in society has not led to their emancipation from the chains of poverty. It has not even succeeded in the simple matter of raising literacy rates (a seemingly impenetrable problem).

It is common knowledge that the higher the quality of a child's education, the higher the prospects of his or her future employment will be. Consequently, there will be a greater likelihood that parents will send their children to school and the fewer children they will have in the first place. Why fewer children? Because they will be more inclined to put their eggs in fewer baskets due to their confidence that their children will be educated well and thus grow up to be successful and have the means to support them in their old age. It will no longer be necessary to go through the considerable aggravation, health risk and expense of having so many children, each one of whom has to be supported in their formative years. In effect, the uncertainty that results in large families will be replaced by a quiet confidence that will result in smaller families.

In Pakistan, population birth rates are especially high in the poorest segments of society. The reason lies not in the ignorance of the poor but in their wisdom. The broken state education systems, the rampant unemployment, and the economic stagnation lead to this atmosphere of uncertainty. This compels the poor to have as many children as possible in an attempt to safeguard their own futures and it is the most realistic decision they could make under the circumstances. But tragically, the children they have are mostly unable to break out of the vicious cycle of poverty.

Breaking this cycle should be one of the foremost priorities of any government. The social and economic problems that have proven to be such an imponderable enigma to planners for decades *can* be solved. But it will require the removal of spurious assumptions. We must discard the excuses of excessive population along with State driven family planning initiatives. These should be recognised for the instruments of diversion that they are. The government should instead concentrate its efforts and available resources on creating a national environment that will enable every single member of society to reach the full limits of their potential.

The problems of the masses cannot justly be solved by simply limiting their size. The core of the problem lies in the languishing of economic activity which prevents increases in income and living standards. Only by reversing our socialistic trends can we stimulate the amount of economic enterprise that will enable the poverty stricken masses to advance. But once and for all, let us make clear, our people are our greatest asset. Their numbers must never be compromised for the sake of political expediency.

12

ON CORRUPTION

"Fascism should rightly be called Corporatism as it is a merger of State and corporate power."

Benito Mussolini

It is a matter of enormous regret that unethical practices are endemic in Pakistani society - so endemic in fact, that they are generally accepted as the standard way of doing things. However, our people are not to blame - mostly they are innocent participants in a *system* that is inherently broken. We all endure an atmosphere where bribery has become part and parcel of daily life. From corporatist graft at the highest levels of State to the palm greasing of petty officials, the issue is now so mundane that people are now desensitised to it and will seldom raise an eyebrow. The level of demoralisation is now so severe that some do not even acknowledge it as an evil. In a system where sleaze is par for the course, can there be any deliverance?

Although we may try to appeal to the moral conscience of the people, the vast majority of our citizens are not deliberately immoral. In fact, they are the biggest victims of a farcical state of affairs where the administrative, beaurocratic and legal system is so wrecked that people must endure bribery simply to get by. These words are not meant to justify bad actions, yes, many are wilful and must correct themselves, but the truth is that most are compelled to indulge in this evil due to grievous circumstances.

Certainly, we must continue to encourage people to refuse to yield to the temptations that corruption invites them to, but the root of the problem lies not with our interactions with minor clerks who take measly bribes in exchange for favours in our towns and cities, but in the vaunted halls of power in Islamabad. It is the government itself at the highest levels that has set the precedent and entrenched itself in immorality. Having polluted the national moral fibre, it has fuelled the widespread belief that these lower moral standards are now acceptable.

If we analyse the occurrence and incidence of corruption across the world, we find patterns. Countries that are mired in corruption tend to be those that are less economically and politically free. They are burdened with rapacious governments and beaurocratic apparatuses that no individual or business can escape. The rule of law in such nations is applied haphazardly, with one rule for the well-connected and another for the helpless. The people must endure and suffer almost absurd levels of State-led interventions into their lives, with nowhere to turn; no court, no authority, no agency able or willing to defend their rights.

This is only too true of Pakistan: a country which, tragically, is ranked all too highly in the 'most corrupt nation' lists that are frequently compiled by independent bodies. But this comes as no surprise to us. Through the enormous powers that their power-grabbing policies allow them to accumulate, the political and beaurocratic elites in Pakistan are the ultimate kleptocrats. Not only do they soak up bribes in an unabashed manner, for many, it is their sole motivation for chasing power.

We are facing a crisis that most commentators cannot even correctly diagnose, let alone remedy. The media calls for action and change - but in the wrong direction. Calls are made for 'reforms' to deal with the mess and it is often said that if we only enacted more rules and regulations, established more checks and balances, and enforced the existing law more strictly, the masses could be assured that the malady was being cured.

Perhaps then, it is assumed, ethical behaviour would return to government. Apparently, new leaders would emerge with spotless records and virtuous habits. A nice thought, but very wrong. It is this kind of liberalism, this kind of woolly and wishful thinking which has ruined the moral fabric of our nation for so long. Where there is no rule of law, only fools pass more legislation. Our existing legal system has failed us. It has become the laughing stock of the world, barely able to protect the rights of our Supreme Court justices, never mind the common man. What's more, our morally corrupt 'legal code' has perpetrated more injustices on our hapless people than any tyrant could possibly dream of.

True reform is impossible unless we realise that our colonial era English Common Law functions in a moral vacuum and in total defiance of natural and divine edict. Writing yet more Western rules and passing yet more Western laws will do nothing but prolong the tyranny. Almost every injustice inflicted on us, whether it be physical, social, economic or spiritual, is sanctioned, even 'legalised' by a system of law that is so beyond the pale that it can only be described as a codified system of deliberate oppression.

In spite of being physically liberated from the colonial oppressor's decades ago, the legacy of British imperialism has remained to this day, in the form of what I call 'brown-sahib imperialism'. These modern day imperialists are the rotten detritus left behind when the British sailed away. As the remnants of the lowest dregs of our society, the collaborators of the time, they unquestioningly and slavishly manifest Western ideals through and through. This in spite of their Muslim names and Muslim appearances. They are nothing more than puppets - puppets whose strings extend to London and Washington.

They will not acknowledge the ideological nature of our country. Instead, despite the mounting evidence of the failure of all foreign ideologies in Pakistan, they persist in chasing Western rainbows - advocating Western inspired solutions to our Western inspired problems. This has never worked, and it never will. No amendment to our English law, no statute, and no regulation will emancipate our nation from the evil of corruption. In fact, it will only further stimulate corrupt activities. The more the pointless laws, rules, legislation and regulations, the greater the potential for bent beaurocrats and ministers to ply for bribes when extorting innocent people. Each meaningless new form, licence and signature requirement only further demoralises us.

Initiatives to combat corruption are often heralded by State spin doctors, but even these cosmetic attempts to shrink corruption are enacted by the very same people who have the most to gain from its continued occurrence. Our politicians may pay lip service to the idea out of public pressure and concern, but 'anti-corruption' drives only force corruption deeper underground and push the money further under the table. Corporations will always look to buy influence, beaurocrats will always seek to entrench power, and vampiric politicians will always want to fill their pockets. There is far too much at stake for them to simply walk away.

The fact is that our socialistic system and bankrupt legal code encourages corporatist and lobbyist vultures to flock to the corridors of authority to cite the 'public interest' in promoting their selfish causes. They grease political and beaurocratic palms and underwrite the passing of legislation that enriches them and marginalises their competitors. Plundering the wealth of the people of Pakistan is a sport for these rogues. We all know this is what goes on. Like a rotten carcass attracting flies and maggots of every kind, this is the inevitable practical result of an interventionist government.

Wherever the freedom of the people is undermined and the State is free to abuse its unchecked power, we find the scandals of the age. This corruption is a natural consequence of the system. It cannot be cured by passing more regulations and more 'anti-corruption' ordinances. We all know these things are a whitewash. How often are corrupt politicians or beaurocrats brought to brook for high-ranking crimes? Hardly ever. But no surprise here. Even the likes of Judas Iscariot would escape prosecution for treason under our laws. Yet the traitors amongst our political ranks are ten a penny. There can be no redemption for our so-called legal code now. It is a system that haemorrhages credibility by the day.

Perhaps it is only when we are plunged into a deep economic crisis and when the parasites have almost bled the people's wealth dry, that we will finally wake up. We can only hope that we all come to our senses sooner. As inflation destroys the wealth of the ordinary family, and regulations cripple business and employment opportunities, the economic pie is starting to shrink. All the more reason for politicians in the nest of vipers we call the National Assembly to snatch a piece while they still can.

This is the system that over the years has indebted our people and our future generations to the tune of jaw-dropping amounts of money through criminally irresponsible and wasteful borrowing and spending. It has been encouraged by successive administrations, abused by the avaricious banking-industrial complex and underwritten by the powerful corporatist elites who have gorged themselves as the primary recipients of the largesse. Through contacts, lobbying and nepotism, they have risen and accumulated enormous wealth at the expense of those who endure a daily struggle to survive.

This is not a free market. This is not free enterprise at work. There is no level playing field here. The parasitic corporations who connive for money and favours in Islamabad are of the opinion that producing and selling products and services that people want is a fool's pursuit. Instead, buying influence to make a fast buck is far more lucrative than working, investing and producing for an honest living. We have seen the money involved in their sleaze grow larger and larger. The problem is aggravated by an ignorant media that eggs on the government to spend and interfere more and more. As far as the media is concerned, politicians simply cannot do enough to tax and spend the nation to prosperity.

This path can only lead to what economist Friedrich von Hayek described as *"the road to serfdom."* We are well and truly on that road. The dangers inherent in this flawed thinking are still being reaped today. Public expenditure is out of control as shown by the budget being in constant deficit year after year. The nation is living far beyond its means, with our politicians unashamedly signing Faustian pacts with foreign powers to sell their souls for a few shekels. They think nothing of being the puppets of foreign enemies who would consider their greatest triumph to be the destruction of our country. How much longer can we afford to mortgage our future for the benefit of these profiteering traitors, the Judas Iscariot's of our time?

* * * * *

The solutions explored in this text are by no means theoretical or hypothetical. They are proven. Islamic free enterprise speaks for itself and requires no bogus propaganda in its favour. No-one can deny that the free enterprise model, hand in hand with the rule of Shariah was the economic environment that propelled the glory of Islamic civilisation for centuries. It is a natural, divinely sanctioned framework that provides, as ever, by far the most fair, humanitarian and effective solution. Those who advocate an imported Westernised approach to solving our deep-set problems are far off the mark. The facts have proven them wrong time and time again across the world and in virtually every circumstance.

Yet the Western shills in our midst still clutch at straws and blame the 'incorrect application' of socialism. This is a canard. When trying to implement a flawed ideology, we will only encounter flaw after flaw. For many years, the State has floundered under abysmally inefficient public administration, lacklustre State-owned enterprises and widespread corruption. It is because many supposedly enlightened individuals have believed, and continue to believe, that it is not beyond the wit of beaurocrats sitting in air-conditioned public buildings to regulate and intervene in the lives of tens of millions of disparate souls.

We are inescapably bound by the arbitrary decisions of those who have little knowledge of the realities of our daily lives. The regulations imposed have done little to improve our condition and have instead been destructive towards lives and businesses, resulting in less enterprise, fewer jobs, and the entrenchment of poverty. Excessive regulation has fuelled the fires of desperation, immorality and helplessness that have engulfed our society. By dampening all legitimate means to get ahead, these measures have criminalised otherwise honest and hardworking people by often forcing them to resort to bribery, nepotism and theft. When even the simplest activities such as opening a businesses or buying property take months or even years, it is no surprise that honest people are forced to operate outside the law.

In a country like Pakistan, which has weak checks and balances on the operations of State institutions, layers of red tape only provide further cover for bribe taking and graft. Corruption occurs best in places where there are many loopholes, where decisions are passed from pillar to post, and where multiple stamps and authorisations are needed for a single approval. This approval may be for a simple, honest and well-intentioned purpose on the part of the individual or organisation that needs it, but the greater the number of hoops to be jumped through, the greater will be the opportunities for corrupt officers to extort bribes for easier passage. Whatever it takes to 'fast-track' the process and earn extra rupees at the expense of a despairing soul.

Yet even though such interference should only occur when absolutely necessary, the number of regulations being churned out of Islamabad and the provincial capitals constitutes a booming sector of its own. When will politicians realise that simply *decreeing* that the world must be a better place, does not make it so?

Regulation does have a role to play in economic life, but a modest and passive one. We need to come to terms with the fact that our advancement will not accelerate through the increasing number of man-made rules imposed on the citizenry, but by the measure of our freedom from interference and dominance from the State. Not only does the current penchant for regulating everything disrupt and misallocate scarce resources, but there are regulations in place that are not even enforceable, and whose positive effects exist only in the imaginations of the politicians who ratify them.

Nothing is seemingly out of reach of the States grasp. By erecting so many barriers that need to be surmounted, the government makes it all the more difficult for entrepreneurs and citizens to get their ideas off the ground and start creating and spreading wealth and jobs for the country. Each extra line of pointless sanction incurs more and more damage on wealth-creating activity, and thus lessens the benefit to society. This leads to distortions, and the conduct of activity that is not in the optimal interest of the country as a whole.

The historical record is clear. Government is not a solution to, but a *precursor* to corruption. The best performers on the corruption index where Pakistan does so poorly are those countries that employ mostly free market policies, establish the rule of law and have the least government intervention. Wherever the State has exerted a light and minimal touch on the economic affairs of the citizens and businesses of a nation, growth has been significantly higher, corruption has been minimal, and greater prosperity has spread to all classes and sectors of the populace. The astounding levels of growth and the lack of corruption in countries such as Hong Kong and Singapore are based on governments that impose only the lightest touch, and yet impose the rule of law on all bar none.

Contrary to popular belief, the market system is not by nature corrupt. It is neither ethical, nor unethical. It is simply a mechanism for allocating scarce resources to their optimal uses. But if it is usurped and hijacked by special interests, the market system is not incorruptible. Corruption is caused by the deliberate or accidental collusion between a powerful government and parasitic corporations. This is a phenomenon that Mussolini proudly described as *corporatism*. It is no coincidence that his fascism was merely an ultra-nationalistic variant of socialism.

No surprise here - socialism, corporatism and economic fascism are different names for the same thing. They are practically indistinguishable. The solution to this systemic corruption is to strip politicians of their unchecked powers, the powers that make them so fruitful a target for corporate bosses. Separating the powerful from the power-seeking is the logical thing to do. To quote Adam Smith, such people, *"...seldom meet together, even for merriment and diversion, but the conversation ends in a conspiracy against the public..."*

If left to its own devices, even when things go wrong, a *truly* free market, unburdened by corporate-political collusion has a remarkable capacity to correct itself. In fact, a real market driven economy actively weeds out corruption. Malpractice, theft, cover-ups, and fraud are soon exposed. Companies that indulge in such evils are eventually found out and their customers, partners and shareholders soon lose confidence and desert them. Businesses and employers who fail to live up to the expectations of consumers do not last for very long and are soon replaced by others that can deliver.

In the market, consumer confidence is critical, and sane managers will protect their reputations at considerable cost to themselves. The bedrock of voluntary cooperation and trade is mutual trust. Unethical practices may be covered up for a short time, but sooner or later those that try to deceive suddenly find that their sales, profits and market share implode. The consequences of fraudulent practices are swift and lethal. It is not just the fittest that survive, but those that are honest. Quite simply, one of the greatest forces we can deploy against corruption is the pressure of free enterprise itself.

Corruption causes immense anxiety and despair for ordinary Pakistanis. It will continue, unless the wholesale reform of our economic, monetary, and legal system is not accomplished. So far our people have traded their right to independence, economic freedom and self reliance for the possibility of government 'benevolence', only for it never to arrive. If only they had known that it never would. It is vitally important that the people of the nation realise that regulation is not a cure for all ills, and that the free market is not a diabolical invention designed to subdue them. It is time for people and the media to stop looking to the 'demi-god' State to solve their problems. So far this has been a costly policy.

To counter the prolific corruption around us, tinkering around the edges of our English Common Law is not a solution, not even close. The socialist, secularist propagandists have done their work well, but they must be countered. If we wish to cleanse our house, we must cleanse our hearts first. The only solution is to reject the status quo and instead create the conditions for the spread of speedy and certain justice at all levels via the application of Shariah. This is the only framework of social and economic life that creates a just and optimal distribution. It is a mechanism of divine law which no man-made legal code can possibly replace. It is the only road to the salvation of our nation. To rephrase von Hayek, it is *"the road to freedom."*

13

ON TRADE

"My guiding principle will be justice and complete
impartiality, and I am sure that with your support and cooperation, I can look forward to Pakistan becoming one of the
greatest nations of the world."

Quaid-e-Azam

The issue of foreign trade is perhaps one of the most
discussed, debated and controversial economic issues of
modern times. Opinions are often confidently expressed, yet
many are misinformed about the economic theory and practice.
There is perhaps no other national concern that is so clouded
with mistruth, falsity and misguided belief. The media plays a
role here, as pundits and commentators are always keen to
stress the apparent harm that free commerce between nations
does to the common man. This opinion has become
conventional wisdom and is rarely challenged. Politicians too,
display an astounding lack of responsibility as they perpetuate
the same myths. The danger lies in the intensity in which they
do so, as it is difficult for an unschooled person to resist
adopting the same bias.

For the political elite though, this pursuit is probably by no
means the result of their simple ignorance. No doubt they must
find it convenient to manipulate and pander to public

prejudices. By doing so, they can more easily enact protectionist trade policies that favour their corporate darlings. But the astounding level of naiveté on this issue has done great injury to the economic vitality of the nation. For many decades, the economy has endured high tariffs and protectionist policies that have crippled growth and productivity while propping up undeserving political cronies and corporatist leeches.

We should realise that trade and commerce is something that should be encouraged and not dampened. A voluntary trade that occurs through mutual consent benefits both parties. This is the case whether trade occurs locally or across international borders. Nobody would expect certain cities or provinces to impose tariffs on goods and services that cross their respective borders, yet the idea that trade between two nations is sometimes harmful to one party has become a commonly held notion. The myth of exploitation is something that must be debunked for the benefit of the nation. *In any voluntary exchange, buyer and seller must both gain. If one of them did not, the exchange would simply not take place.* In honest trade there are no losers - everyone wins.

Unfortunately for the first few decades of Pakistan's existence, its policy makers, keen to emulate their socialist comrades all over the world, attempted to institute a policy known as 'import-substitution' industrialization. This was a 'protectionist' trade policy based on the misguided premise that a country should attempt to substitute products which it imports (mostly finished goods), with locally produced products. It meant that very high tariffs were placed on imports to discourage them as much as possible. This was done with the aim to encourage industrialisation. However, the policy achieved precisely the opposite effect, failing to expand or deepen industrial growth. It resulted in inferior and more costly domestic substitutes for products that were readily available on world markets.

The objective of creating an atmosphere of 'autarky' and 'self sufficiency' failed spectacularly as competitor nations raced ahead in economic growth. The domestic industries in Pakistan that resulted were shoddy, inefficient and obsolete - totally unable to compete at an international level. The policy has done long term damage. Even today, Pakistan, in spite of being a major world nation, has no internationally renowned companies that operate in the global marketplace.

The attempts by the State to encourage and selectively support some industries while suppressing others was based on the foolish notion that we can be self-sufficient in the production of all goods and services. But the inevitable low quality of products that resulted from such an irrational policy was totally ignored. Self-sufficiency is a foolhardy aim and there is no legitimate or sensible reason why it should ever be attempted.

It is unfathomable that it is still considered acceptable for politicians and media pundits to speak about self-sufficiency as if it is actually desirable. Would these people not be considered lunatics if they suggested that Lahore or Rawalpindi could gain by being self-sufficient in the production of food, or that a tiny village should restrict imports from outside its village limits and instead build its own electrical products?

It makes no sense for an individual, family, city, province or country to make everything they will need in their daily lives all by themselves. It is when we specialise in certain tasks and activities and trade the results of our labour and capital in exchange for other things that we gain from living together in communities. But surely it can be no surprise that phrases such as self-sufficiency are commonly banded about by populist politicians.

Self-sufficiency smacks of senseless old-school ultra-nationalism, and it is a mode of thinking that should be abandoned. Preventing trade with other nations for the sake of self-sufficiency results in a lower standard of living. It means that individuals and businesses are unable to specialise and benefit from selling their goods and services and buying the products of others. International trade extends the division of labour across national boundaries, resulting in even greater potential efficiencies. Clearly, we are confused about the very nature of trade. The trade that occurs between the five provinces or between cities is never a subject of discussion, but trade across international borders suddenly sparks controversy.

In reality, there is no difference in the rationale behind the national division of labour, and the international division of labour. It is the *law of comparative advantage* that illustrates why the international division of labour is so beneficial to all participants. It states that a country can improve its welfare by specialising in the most efficient areas of production open to it. These are those areas in which it has a 'comparative advantage' over other nations. The most efficient areas of production are those areas in which a country's productivity *relative* to other areas is greatest. This does not necessarily mean the areas in which a country is more efficient than *all* other countries.

Some say that poor countries inherently have no comparative advantage in producing anything, and therefore cannot benefit from trade. But this is unfounded - every nation has a comparative advantage in something because some of its industries will be relatively more efficient than others, even if *all* of its industries are more inefficient then the countries it is trading with. So, the law of comparative advantage means that even a country which is the worst at producing everything will still benefit from free trade. This is because it allows the inefficient country to specialise in what it is relatively poor at producing rather than in what it is *even poorer* at producing. This optimises the use of its scarce resources to maximum benefit.

Consider how even the most unskilled labourers benefit from working and trading their labour in a competitive market economy. Quite simply, they are able to specialise in what they do best and so gain from it. It is far more convenient for a labourer to earn a wage through his specialty and then pay for all the goods and services he needs that are produced by other skilled individuals. Far easier and efficient to do this rather then expend time and effort to acquire all the necessary skills to produce all such goods himself.

Conversely, a highly skilled rocket scientist, even if he could do a labourers work more efficiently than our labourer, would also have a comparative advantage in rocketry. But even if he was *significantly* more efficient then our labourer in labouring, his time and resources are obviously scarce, in which case it is better for him to specialise in rocketry and have someone else do his unskilled work: our labourer. Thus both parties benefit from a potential trade. In the same way, even a country that is highly industrialised and advanced benefits from trading with an inefficient and poor nation, and the poor nation benefits too. Both nations have a comparative advantage in something, and this is where they are likely to specialise in a free market.

The comparative advantage that a country or an individual may have in a particular industry or activity at any given point in time can only be determined through the function of price. A workers wage is the price of his labour, and it is the level of wages and prices that signal employers and firms about the viability of pursuing a particular line of activity or production. The problem with government intervention is that it always distorts prices and wages. These distortions increase the value of some profits and wages but decrease the value of others. This results in a channelling of scarce resources into areas where the individual, business, or even country does not have a comparative advantage. This obviously reduces the level of productivity in the economy and impacts on growth, damaging the welfare of the people.

In spite of the protestations of special interests or ignorant politicians and media, it is a universal truth that barriers to legitimate trade only serve to harm an economy. But why do these barriers remain in place? Because there are always individuals and businesses that gain from a policy. Their gain comes at the expense of the rest in society, but they fervently argue their case in favour of protectionism or legislation that would protect them and compromise their competitors. As they often have the legislators in their pockets, they are often successful. Of course they do not explicitly declare their self-interest, they always couch their arguments in terms of the 'national interest'. In reality though, the businesses that are preserved when such policies are instituted are those whose labour and resources could be more productively and efficiently employed elsewhere.

This chicanery adversely affects the common man. Government interventions in trade, international or otherwise, prevent the most efficient division of labour and thus force consumers to pay higher prices for a lower quality. This is not trivial. In Pakistan, because of barriers to trade, we pay far more than we should have to for practically every good or service we purchase. The distortions in efficiency that result from import and export tariffs directly impact on the nations standard of living, leaving it much lower than it otherwise would be.

If such barriers and regulations were abolished, the economy would be significantly more productive, mainly because industries would align themselves through the energy of the free market to specialise in those areas and sectors of production where we have a comparative advantage. This would lead to significantly less wastage of scarce resources on inefficient industries that simply would not survive without government shelter and restrictions to legitimate trade. As a relatively poor and underdeveloped economy, Pakistan has an enormous amount to gain from international trade, and the greater efficiencies that can result from it. These are the efficiencies that are so desperately needed to shape highly capable industries that will blossom and expand, creating wealth and employment for all.

* * * * *

There is a great hue and cry in the media about the balance of payments, and whether the nation is running trade deficits or surpluses, assuming that one of the two things is favourable and the other not. Neither is true. The balance of payments simply describes the pattern of trade. It is made up of the current account and the capital account. The current account measures the flow of goods and services, and the capital account measures the flow of funds and financial assets. The balance of payments always balances. With every trade that is transacted, if goods or services flow one way, then money and financial assets inevitably flow in the other. Overall, for every current account deficit, there is a corresponding capital account surplus.

Every province, city, family, or even individual has a balance of trade, but there is no logical or practical reason for ever knowing what it is. Yet the existence of international borders means that statistics are collected for the flow of trade across national boundaries. But these measurements only describe the pattern of trade and we cannot surmise anything else from them. Regardless of the opinions of some commentators, the shape or direction of the trade flow itself tells us nothing about whether an economy is successful or not. All that matters is that the trade is free and not coerced or distorted by government.

By definition, all trade that is voluntarily transacted and legitimate is a good thing. If it was not, it would not have been agreed to by both parties. But some say that a trade deficit is a bad thing, and that a surplus is preferable. But if a business or a nation as a whole has sold assets to buy foreign goods, is there any reason to believe that this is a bad thing? Why would both parties have agreed to such a transaction if it was a bad deal for one of them?

The preference for trade surpluses and the wringing of hands over trade deficits makes little sense. After all, both patterns of trade are consistent with both low and high growth. At the time of writing, Pakistan currently runs a current account deficit. Contrary to a lot of the nonsense written about such things, it is not a deep cause for concern: the United States ran a current account deficit for most of the nineteenth century, during which time it was rapidly industrialising and was the most dynamic economy in history.

Regardless, some talk about a balance of payments crisis as if it is something that we should be seriously worried about. Some perspective is needed. There is no crisis. In reality, the term 'crisis' is only coined by agitators to explain the failure of government to sufficiently intervene in the foreign exchange markets in order to fulfil a political objective, this normally being an increase in exports in order to induce 'export-led growth'. Here, the government will attempt to actively intervene in the foreign exchange markets to buy foreign currency and sell

Rupees, effectively depressing the price of the Rupee and so making Pakistani exports cheaper to foreigners.

But exports are not necessarily better then imports. The people benefit enormously from imports. They can drive Japanese cars, buy Brazilian radios and eat quality food from all over the world. Imports allow consumers to buy a huge array of higher quality goods from other countries at lower prices than they would pay if they were restricted to only buying domestic goods. It is imports that improve the quality of life of the people, all of whom are consumers. Once our exports are sent across our borders, they are of no use as they cannot be consumed by us. In fact, exports should be considered the price the nation pays to be able to afford useful imported goods.

There can be no balance of payments problem as long as the price of the Rupee in terms of any other international currency is determined in a free market by voluntary transactions. There should be no government intervention to artificially reduce the value of the Rupee. This simple effect of a ludicrous policy of exchange rate manipulation is that Pakistan expends massive amounts of foreign reserves in order to make Pakistani exports cheaper. Effectively, this is a subsidy for foreigners.

It is a nonsensical policy. We have millions living in extreme poverty in our nation and instead of caring for them we are spending our scarce resources on subsidising the consumerism of foreign peoples. For years, Pakistan's government has intervened on a massive scale in order to depress the price of the Rupee. In the process we have squandered vast sums of the nation's money. More importantly, this intervention has compromised the efficiency of our industries and has reduced our productivity and level of employment. The practice has prevented free-floating prices and exchange rates from performing their proper function.

Often the case is made that we should place higher tariffs on imports in reciprocation of another country doing so as it is 'protecting' or subsidising its own industries and acting unfairly. But all that this 'cheating' leads to is a misallocation of their (and our) resources. If a foreign government wishes to waste their time by entering into industries and sectors where their productive resources are not being optimally used then that is their problem. We should not be doing the same; in fact we should create a free trade environment and benefit from their subsidies to our consumers.

According to politicians and media commentators, the rationale behind high tariffs on imports is to enable certain domestic industries to be protected from competition from foreign goods which are likely to be better and cheaper. The claim is made that domestic firms cannot be expected to compete with foreign ones. This argument is fallacious. Tariffs against imports keep our domestic industries fat and contented, unexposed to the rigours and positive effects of international competition. As usual, it is the public who are the greatest losers, as they have to make do with high priced and poor quality domestic goods. This coupled with monetary inflation does an enormous amount of damage to the average standard of living.

Equally pernicious is the fact that our scarce land, labour and capital is tied up in sectors of the economy in which we have no comparative advantage. Imports do not reduce the productivity of the domestic economy, they simply encourage specialisation in more productive activities. If the manner in which our resources are utilised is uncompetitive because our domestic industries are filling gaps in the market which high tariffs prevent imports from filling themselves, then the outcome is not favourable at all.

The biggest problem with protectionism is its extremely close link to *corporatism*. When corporations and governments come together to collude, bad things happen for the rest of society. A free market means that the government should have a hands-off policy concerning all trade apart from the illegal variety. But when corporations use their clout in order to influence policy, this is corporatism, and must be strongly condemned and stamped out. When even established industries begin to lose their comparative advantage, they will invariably turn to the State for protection if the State permits it.

Using influence and the vagaries and complexities of legislation, they will whisper sweetly into the ears of politicians in order to establish policies that allow them to profiteer, oppress their competitors, and rob the public through higher prices. Tariffs are a primary form of protection from foreign competition. But protectionism results in domestic consumers being denied the best, cheapest products available and such protection keeps industries alive that would serve better being put out of their misery for the betterment of all.

The protectionist has yet another claim. This is the argument that young and growing industries and sectors need to be protected from the rigorous competition that results from foreign trade - yet another fallacious argument. In a dynamic free market economy with vibrant capital markets and a sound and honest monetary system, businesses that are currently not profitable but may be profitable in the future will have no problems obtaining investment to take them through their infant phase.

The only ones that will fail to raise funds are those deemed to be bad risks and a misallocation of capital. But if the market is not willing to bear the risk then why should the taxpayer? Why should the 'coping classes' be further burdened with the defence and subsidisation of risky industries? The problem with such protectionism is that it only serves to misallocate resources in maintaining industries that do not have a comparative advantage - at the expense of those that do.

It is important to be crystal clear. Regardless of whatever other countries do by way of trade restrictions, the best policy for Pakistan is always to engage in free trade with everyone. Free trade is always mutually beneficial, and barriers to trade are always damaging. It allows us to allocate our resources to their best and optimal applications, and thus raises productivity and living standards. Imports should be welcomed and not discouraged as they increase our quality of life, and exports should not be given preference. But a caveat: not everything labelled 'free trade' actually is.

So-called 'free trade' deals and international blocs such as the WTO and SAFTA do not achieve the benefits of free trade but instead are a threat to the independence of our nation. They are instruments of 'managed' trade that only bring deliberate benefits to certain industries, sectors and assorted special interest groups while transferring power to foreign, unaccountable elites. It is only pseudo free trade that is being pedalled here, after all, how 'free' can the trade possibly be if the agreement comes with thousands of stipulations?

We cannot achieve the full benefits of free trade through corporatist internationally managed trade regimes. These beaurocratic organisations have agreements that are comprised of thousands of pages of minutiae and complicated legalese - all the better to hide protectionist measures for influential special interests and multinational corporations. We should cancel memberships in such parasitic organisations and unilaterally liberalise our trading practices. Greater international trade does not come as a result of governmental cooperation and coordination - it comes as a result of free markets and private initiative.

Recall that only a hundred years ago, there were no restrictions on trade at all. Throughout the history of the Caliphate, people could come and go as they wished. There were no 'visiting visas', manned borders, passports or tariffs to prevent movement and commerce. The segmentation of the Ummah through ultra-nationalism and separatism is only a recent phenomenon. A question arises: these barriers that separate us - have they benefited, or harmed us? Or have they only been imposed on us? Time to go back to basics. We should abolish such barriers without fear.

Free trade is not complicated at all. There are no provisos. It simply implies zero tariffs on all legal imports and exports, free floating exchange rates and no clumsy central bank interventions. The dynamism and efficiencies it generates boosts economic growth significantly - proven to be up to several percentage points a year. For Pakistan, it is a catalyst that we desperately need. Let there be no delay. It is time for us to follow the example of high-growth free trading giants like China and Singapore and finally act in the interests of the Pakistani people. We need free trade now.

14

ON CREDIT

"It is well enough that people of the nation do not
understand our banking and monetary system, for if
they did, I believe there would be a revolution before
tomorrow morning."

Henry Ford

The curse of price inflation haunts us. There seems to be no respite for the common man. Everything is becoming more and more expensive and yet nobody can come up with a satisfactory explanation. This phenomenon is causing acute pain to millions of households who are struggling to survive on what little money they have. We are finding that our static incomes are failing to keep up with the massive increases in the cost of living. The price of food, fuel, energy, housing and everything else is rocketing far beyond our means to keep up. The middle classes are being wiped out. God help us, the poorest are in an even worse state. But why does this happen? Why don't rupees go as far as they used to?

It is really much simpler than most people imagine it to be. The rupee, like the dollar and every other currency in existence, is a mere political currency, unredeemable for any real asset. The rupee is not a certificate of real wealth, but a 'note of credit', based on a trust and promise from the central bank and politicians that it will retain its future value. The currency is not based on any real and valuable commodity like gold or silver. It is based on nothing.

Depending on the whim of the State Bank of Pakistan, extra rupees are printed and issued to pay for shortfalls in the government budget or to pay off debt. Remember, these notes are just pieces of paper with ink designs on them and for the State Bank to print more is an easy matter. But every extra rupee issued diminishes the value of every other rupee in the economy and thus weakens its buying power for the public. Hence goods and services become more expensive with time. In effect, this 'fiat' monetary system destroys the wealth of the poor and middle classes who suffer most from price rises.

When this inflationary money is created out of thin air, it is injected into the economy through private and government owned banks in the form of credit and new paper notes. Through the 'fractional reserve banking' process, the new money is multiplied even further and lent for bank profits based on interest rate returns from borrowers. These credit markets keep business and consumer activity churning over. The key to the manipulation of the system is the ability of the State Bank of Pakistan to artificially price the base interest rate.

A low interest rate means cheap credit, an increased money supply, more borrowing, and a consumer boom. A higher interest rate results in more expensive credit, a contraction in the money supply leading to less borrowing, and a slowdown in growth. 'Monetary policy' comes in the form of central bank decisions that are euphemistically known as 'loosening and tightening', where interest rate cuts mean loosening and hikes mean tightening. It sounds eerily similar to having a noose around someone's neck.

It is not such a bad analogy. By changing base interest rates, the State Bank of Pakistan can constrict or ease the financial situation for the entire country. Thus an immense amount influence over the lives and properties of hundreds of millions is vested into the hands of a tiny group of individuals who are politically motivated in their actions. It is no surprise then, that prior to elections, politicians will pressurise the State Bank governor to lower interest rates to supply cheap credit to the masses and thus fuel an artificially generated 'feel-good' boom.

The problem is that inevitably, every boom eventually turns to bust, causing havoc for millions of ordinary families. But since when did the interests of the ordinary people ever get in the way of short-term political expediency? In The Communist Manifesto, Karl Marx laid out his ten tenets of extreme socialism. His fifth is especially relevant: *"Centralization of credit in the hands of the state, by means of a national bank with state capital and an exclusive monopoly."* Why the global monetary system is based on the degenerate ideas of this man is a complete mystery. Yet here we are.

When interest rates (the price of money or credit) are changeable at the whim of the central bank, booms and busts are the unavoidable result. No matter how hard the State Bank tries to engineer 'safe landings' for the economy and avoid recessions by tinkering with the base interest rate, they always happen. The problem is that there are too many variables involved and these people are only under the illusion that they know what they are doing, besides which, when the economy goes awry they can always pass the buck and blame 'external factors' or 'global conditions'.

Interest rate cuts and cheap credit is always seen as the quick and easy answer. When interest rates are artificial and credit is distributed according to a arbitrary rate that is lower than a 'natural' equilibrium market rate, i.e. if monetary policy is 'loosened', excess credit often engulfs the economy, creating 'bubbles'. This gives the illusion of prosperity. But in reality the new found wealth is concentrated in the hands of very few through the 'bubble' stock market, 'bubble' house price increases, and the profiteering corporations who have direct credit lines with the government.

Only a minority of the population benefit through cheap loans, stock market bubbles, or corporatist subsidies. The vast majority only suffer the consequences of the profligacy. The apparent new-found prosperity in the form of shiny new cars on the streets and new shopping malls is therefore not based on real production and wealth but in fact on mountains of cheap debt, and as every debtor knows, the bills always catch up with you in the end.

* * * * *

Avoidable problems arise when our government gets involved in placing cheap loans directly in the hands of people who are probably not creditworthy. It often even supplies credit to those who would have secured credit privately had they not been tempted by the discounted interest rates they are being charged by the State. But then beaurocrats need not worry about the realities of commercial transactions. Unlike a private lender who has a vested interest in getting his money back, the State has no such incentive. The State distributes taxpayer's money like confetti for political objectives, and supplements it with new money fresh from the central banks printing presses.

In the minds of politicians - industries, farmers and individuals simply cannot get enough credit. The amount of credit supplied by banks and other lenders is never enough, and there is a notion that there are gaps in the credit market, whereby unfortunate individuals and business are not receiving credit even though in the minds of politicians, they deserve it. When a politician has one eye on public appeasement and the other on a future election, the result tends towards very bad policies. The argument is made that it would be in the interests of the national economy if some people were given easy loans. Complaints are made that interest rates are too high, or that people who have poor credit histories cannot get the loans they need to get ahead.

What results is the creation of government lending institutions that lend money to various groups who would otherwise not get credit. This money is often lent on a very favourable basis to the individual, whether in the form of direct government credit or a full guarantee of private loans. Credit is offered below market rates and with easy payment terms. But unfortunately, the policy is seriously flawed and short-sighted. Government intervention in the money and credit markets always ends badly, serving to distort the natural course of the economy. Government 'help' should be just as feared as government hostility.

All honest loans must eventually be repaid: that should be a given. Credit equals debt, and any proposals or policies that succeed in increasing the volume of credit in the economy actually increase the burden of debt. Private loans and debt from private banks based on the credit status of individuals and businesses are a natural part of the functioning of the economy. We need not have any issue with such privately acquired credit, as long as it is lawful and compliant with Shariah.

Private car loans, mortgages, and loans for household items are fine. The debt that is a problem is the credit supplied by the *government* or some government affiliated institution that offers loans at discount rates out of taxpayer's funds and newly printed credit supplied from the State Bank. This type of credit distorts the market grievously to the detriment of national productivity and the interests of the common man.

These loans are often designed to provide capital to businesses and farmers to facilitate the purchase of equipment, stock, property or services necessary for their operation and expansion. They may be 'start-up' loans designed to jump-start businesses through the injection of cheap capital. At first, people may have little or no objection to the thought of the State facilitating loans to those who clearly need them.

Why not help a poor farmer out by giving him credit and a helping hand to pull him out of harsh poverty? Is it not cruel to allow someone to live in poverty when they can so easily be helped? Besides which, by helping him, we help his family and his whole community. Another argument is that the loan costs very little to the taxpayer in comparison to the benefits that will be derived from it. After all, the loan will be paid back in time. The case in favour of government intervention does seem convincing and it seems a humanitarian solution to a difficult problem.

But it is still wrong, and here is why. We fail to realise that this kind of credit is already provided on a daily basis by the private sector. If someone is creditworthy, and has only the fraction of the capital necessary to start a new project or business or wishes to expand his existing operations, a private lender will have no problem lending him the necessary funds as long as he can prove his creditworthiness. Often companies have finance departments that cater exclusively for the provision of such credit to potential customers.

If someone wishes to purchase equipment or services, they are often furnished with the necessary finance plan that will allow them to do so, with payments being paid through the earnings of the project or through part ownership of it. Shariah-based finance offers many solutions to this problem and private lenders do this all the time; in fact, they are well-aware that any capital that sits idle with them is not earning them a return. They welcome the opportunity to utilise their funds.

Here lies the rub. There is a profound difference between private loans issued to people and taxpayer subsidised loans issued to the same. The purpose of a loan is to risk and bring in a return. A private lender will risk his *own* funds (or funds entrusted to him for which he is trustee), so naturally he will take every care to ensure that the borrower will make good. He will make comprehensive credit checks, review past borrowing patterns, inspect business plans, even interview neighbours and family to check for honesty of character of the borrower and perhaps much more. In short, he will make a calculated decision on whether to lend based on the established creditworthiness of the individual or business.

This begs the question: does the government go through such rigorous measures to ensure that taxpayer's funds that are lent in such a manner are paid back in full? If the answer is yes, then this in a single stroke abolishes the necessity of government administered credit. There is no reason whatsoever why the government should ever be involved in a service that duplicates what already happens in the private sector. It is a waste of time, taxpayer's funds and resources, indeed, it is nonsensical.

Of course, the answer is in fact no. The government does not go through such rigorous measures because it operates by wholly different standards and has very little incentive to discharge its duties in a responsible manner. Defenders of publicly administered credit contend that the whole purpose of such credit is to present loans to individuals and businesses whom private lending institutions will not service. What they really mean is that they are prepared take levels of risks with taxpayer's money which a private institution would never accept (nor afford).

What is it about taxpayer funds, collected from the sweat and toil of individuals and businesses and entrusted to a supposedly responsible government, which makes them more expendable than private funds? It is a common refrain that it is far easier to waste someone else's money than to waste one's own. But do the principles of responsible lending and the discharge of proper and moral duties not apply to the government? Seemingly not to any Pakistani government we have ever seen.

It is important to analyse the situation of public lending by viewing it in a wider context. The amount of capital in the economy is finite. What is lent to one person cannot be lent to another, and there is a cost to lending capital in a fashion that does not optimise its utilisation. The cost lies in the so-called 'opportunity cost' of not lending the capital to someone more worthy of it, and by worthy, we mean more likely to utilise the capital to maximise returns.

If a man is creditworthy, he will receive credit in the private sector as he should. If he receives it from the State, this means that taxpayer's money is being spent unnecessarily, albeit on a good risk. On the other hand, a person who is deemed in the marketplace as not creditworthy will generally not receive a private loan, because the risk of a default is too great and better risks can be found for lending. If the government intervenes and guarantees a private loan or simply loans money directly, then it is only from a charitable perspective. It is a bad risk, and the cost of taxpayer losses is significant.

Taxpayers may get their money back or more likely they may not, but the government is less concerned about the possibility of a default because it is less accountable than a private lender would be. A private lender making similarly poor lending decisions would soon be overwhelmed by bad debts and go out of business, but a government lender has a continuous stream of new money and an opaque system of accountability.

Not all 'charitable' loans will become bad debts. In some cases they may work out all right and the loans will be returned in full. However, in general, the loans will be greater risks and a great deal of taxpayer's money will be lost. They will be less efficient, more open to abuse and corruption, and resources will be expended that would be better spent in the interests of the people elsewhere.

When the government intervenes in such a way, it affects the average rate of return for all capital and thus 'crowds out' private lenders. When scarce capital is artificially placed in the hands of less trustworthy and less efficient borrowers (however well intentioned), it cannot reach safer borrowers. Capital brings returns, and if government intervention reduces the scale of these returns, by investing in projects of dubious merit, it means that the economy is not being made wealthier, but poorer. We do not miss this extra wealth because we never see it, but we are losing it all the same.

The assumption behind government credit which is not overtly mentioned to the public is that the government should assume risks with hard-earned taxpayer's funds that a private lender would never tolerate. Taxpayer funds are implicitly seen as worth less and thus far more expendable. This leaves beaurocrats and politicians with considerable openings for corruption and nepotism with government credit. If the decisions of beaurocrats are not held to the same standard as those for private lenders, then beaurocrats can take risks with funds that will inevitably lead to a myriad of evils.

We know this has happened and is still happening in Pakistan. Favouritism, nepotism, bribes, scandals - these things help to demoralise society and the national economy, giving signals to borrowers that they don't need a good business plan or project to get ahead, and they don't even need to be creditworthy, rather, they just need a useful contact and a willingness to grease palms. Should we be surprised when excessive State intervention results in such evil?

But for the moral character, honesty and piety of many of our fellow citizens, the situation would be a lot worse. Otherwise, why would more people not take the easier immoral path when the right path is more difficult to tread? Corruption is not endemic in our people - it is the system that is corrupt, and it is the system that must be reformed.

Of course, many people are looking for ways in which to invest their capital, but the only moral course is for lenders to lend in the private sector, and for borrowers to borrow in the private sector. Naturally, mistakes will be made, and some bad debts will result, but that is to be expected. This is the nature of risk. This is life. What we know for certain is that the private sector, if left to its own devices, will take far fewer risks then government lenders will, and there will be no opportunity for brazen corruption and nepotism.

Private lenders must compete for borrowers and they must weigh and calculate the risks of lending carefully. The law of the survival of the fittest applies, and if all capital is funnelled through the private sector and if there is minimal government interference, the very scarce resources of a poor developing country will be optimally utilised rather than much being wasted. Beaurocrats who pass civil service exams and politicians who try to bribe constituents with subsidies and cheap loans are not in a position to allocate the resources of the economy in the most efficient manner. They have other priorities. It is a system of easy credit where excessive risk-taking is rewarded and sensible prudence is punished.

The unintended consequences of government credit are highly detrimental to the health and vitality of the economy as a whole. Just look at the 'credit crunch' that is currently engulfing the world. It originated as the result of the US Government's policies to force banks to provide loans to people who probably could not afford to pay them back. Unsurprisingly, many could not, and the house of cards collapsed.

A government never lends or gives anything to people that it does not take away from others. We see the people who receive the loans, but we do not see those who are denied them even though they were more deserving. Effectively the policy works in a way whereby the risk-prone and unsuccessful are rewarded and subsidised at the expense of those who are successful and prudent. Under some emergency circumstances, there may be some merits to such lending, but in the long run it burdens the economy and causes untold, unforeseen problems.

There is a role for government to play on this issue. The best way to cater for those who are not creditworthy is to strengthen property rights. Capital can be derived from property and ownership, but the beaurocratic mess that surrounds the public land and property record system is something that must be reformed. The process for buying, selling and transferring property is pedantic and cumbersome and many businesses and individuals suffer as a result. It needs to be streamlined to ensure quick and efficient turnaround times.

We should remind ourselves that credit is something that a person has fundamentally. It is based on their assets, character, business acumen and determination. When they ask for financial credit in the form of a loan, they already have the above qualities and assets in excess of the amount for which they are asking. The amount of credit they can receive is based on the accumulated record that they have lived and earned.

They take their credit to a private lender, and when the lender accepts their creditworthiness in good faith, the lender will be pleased to offer him a loan. But the lenders risk is calculated because based on the borrowers record he feels assured to a reasonable degree that he will get his money back. Sometimes he will make a mistake and incur a bad debt, but that is why it is so important to be prudent with all credit when a nation's resources are so scarce. In order to maximise growth, they must be utilised in the most optimal fashion. As the 'credit crunch' has proven, government lending only causes trouble.

The blame lies with a monetary policy that is unfair, elitist and highly disruptive to the interests of the common man. The under-pricing of credit and the inflationary policies of the State Bank are responsible for causing price-rises and bubbles that are created through all lending institutions, public or private. Eventually the post-bubble chickens must come home to roost. The inevitable damage this causes is so widespread and dispersed, that people cannot even understand what the problem is, let alone identify who is to blame. Clearly, the fault lies with the government, which just needs to return to a more moral and Islamic credit and monetary policy.

15

ON POVERTY

"In a country where the sole employer is the State,
opposition means death by slow starvation. The old
principle: who does not work shall not eat, has been
replaced by a new one: who does not obey shall not eat."

Leon Trotsky

With the advent of Islam over fourteen hundred years ago, a new economic order fell into place. It consisted of voluntary economic cooperation: a sound monetary system; freedom of exchange and trade; and the widespread protection of private property. Its fruits came in the form of prosperity, influence, and esteem. A thousand years later, as the Muslim world abandoned these principles and languished, the Western world began implementing what had been forgotten by the East. This order came to be known as 'free enterprise'. Irrespective of how this system is regarded, whether it is admired or disparaged, it is this system that has since conquered mass poverty in the Western world. Conversely, to this day many Muslim nations still find themselves seemingly mired in the disease of scarcity, unable to escape the curse that afflicted their forefathers.

The history of mankind is set against a backdrop of mass poverty. In pre-industrial societies, famine, scarcity, war and pestilence were part of life. In these agricultural economies, cycles of surplus and scarcity were determined by drought, floods, fires and plagues. Economic life was heavily dependent on a handful of primary crops, and because they were grown largely for subsistence, when these crops failed, the consequences were disastrous. Measures for storing surplus crops were crude and the wealth and means required for importing and exporting basic foodstuffs to maintain consistent supplies were not sufficient to prevent large scale shortages.

It was only in the late eighteenth and nineteenth centuries in Europe that circumstances allowed for greater agricultural productivity. Industrialisation resulted in higher crop yields which pushed production above the subsistence threshold. This greater abundance of food helped to sustain an increasing population, and the decreasing reliance on manpower on the farms also led to rural folk heading to the towns and cities for work.

The growing trend of capital accumulation and commerce provided the catalyst for greater prosperity and wealth creation - all underpinned by a philosophy of economic liberty. Ever since, in Western societies and lately in some Eastern ones too, vigorous enterprise and free markets have steadily increased the average income. As these societies have modernised and industrialised, the occasional natural disasters and crises that befall them are more easily absorbed and countered through the blessings of technological progress and wealth.

In advanced economies, poverty is a residual and relative phenomenon that only affects a minority of the citizenry. On the other end of the spectrum, developing countries still have a large proportion of their populations mired in the worst kind of grinding urban and rural deprivation. It is this kind of poverty that concerns us most - *extreme* poverty. This is 'absolute' poverty and is easily measurable and consistent across the world.

Here the poorest are simply unable to provide for their basic material needs on a day to day basis. Food, clean water, shelter, clothing, and healthcare are too often out of their reach. Unfortunately for some, going to sleep on a full stomach in a shelter fit for human habitation is too rare an occurrence. It is difficult to dwell on such chronic human misery, but because it often occurs beyond our vision, we must be reminded of its appalling dimensions to better help us understand why it happens and indeed, why we still allow it to happen.

Every nation has at least some incidence of poverty, but the measurements in advanced countries differ in the respect that in these societies there is little or no poverty of the *extreme* kind. Practically every member of these societies has access to a social safety net that enables them to provide for their minimum comfort. Poverty in these cases is defined in *relative* terms to the rest of society. Because most have a roof over their heads and benefit from clean water, electricity and reasonably plentiful food, poverty is necessarily more nuanced in its definition. It is better termed as the level of *inequality*.

Yet people deemed extremely poor in the West would be considered middle-class if they lived in similar conditions in a poorer country. So in wealthier societies the definition of poverty is often difficult to grasp and is far more subjective. For example, is a family living in Belgium considered poor if they do not own a computer while most other Belgian households do? There will be differing opinions on the matter.

Talking about inequality or 'income disparity' perhaps makes sense in Western countries, but in poorer countries such as Pakistan, where extreme poverty is common, such references are surely redundant. In reality there will always be individuals in a society that are wealthier than others. When the poor are in such desperate need though, does it make any material difference how wealthy the rich are, as long as they are not robbing the poor to become so?

In Pakistan, the constant clamouring over income disparity is a red herring that disguises failures towards the very poorest in society. Instead of positively acting to uplift the state of the extreme poor by using the most tried and tested means, many will seek to assuage our collective failures by diverting attentions and pandering to our worst inclinations toward envy. Shakespeare elegantly described this phenomenon through the mouth of Iago, *"O! beware, my lord, of jealousy; It is the green-ey'd monster which doth mock the meat it feeds on."*

Unfortunately, the profoundly important task of reducing the percentage of the population trapped in extreme poverty is too often neglected by opinion makers and politicians. Instead of focusing sharply on the matter at hand, they pontificate about the perceived widening wealth gap. But in reality there are only two ways to reduce inequality: either the existing *poor can be made richer* or the existing *rich can be made poorer*. Either way, inequality is reduced, but the first way is virtuous (but politically difficult), and the other is ruinous (but politically expedient).

What these misguided folk fail to realise is that while they concentrate on pulling down individuals who have succeeded in society (in an honest and legal manner), they should be more concerned with uplifting the poorest and most dispossessed. But it is easy to see why our politicians prefer the easy option. After all, the law of gravity informs us that it requires less perspiration to pull something down then it does to push something up.

It is socialism that informs this warped thought-process. Throughout Pakistan's history, socialism has been the supreme political and economic ideology. Time and time again, politicians have attempted to manipulate our delicate, nascent economy in order to 'equalise' wealth across society. The real effect though, has been to critically stunt the growth of the economy and entrench the extreme poverty that advocates of the socialism they claim they are trying to eliminate.

Through socialistic policies, an equalised level of income *can* be achieved, but it can only be levelled down. The net result is that the total wealth of the nation is smaller than it otherwise would be. This is precisely the wrong outcome if the intention is to eradicate poverty - it leads to more poverty and not less. Clearly these crude policies hurt the interests and prospects of the poor most of all. But what does it matter to egalitarians if the nation becomes more impoverished as long as everyone is equally impoverished?

As the English saying goes, 'the devil plays the sweetest tunes'. Unfortunately, such populism is often sweet music to the ignorant masses who are too easily beguiled by the seemingly palatable fix that is being offered. As the repeated election victories of socialistic parties has proved, leftist political rhetoric is highly effective. But the facts of history bear witness to the reality of what these people do once they come to office. While they may publicly advocate for greater support for the poor when electioneering, after Election Day, they actively subsidise and bolster an elite few and their favoured corporate interests. Through their largely unchecked powers, they hammer the poor and middle classes while enriching the well-connected and undeserving; all this while cloaking their proposals in the language of equality and fairness.

Apart from Pakistan's economically optimistic decade in the 1960's when growth began to accelerate and poverty decrease, attempts to uplift the dispossessed masses in the remaining period have proved to be largely fruitless. To prove the point, if the growth rates of the 1960's had continued to the present day, the income of the average Pakistani would be at least 80% higher than it is now. Yet instead, the attentions of successive governments toward the welfare of the poor were diverted by petty bickering, feuding and power mongering. Throughout, oft repeated anti-poverty schemes consisted only of wasteful subsidies, price fixing, punitive taxation, and spurious regulation. In spite of the continuous malfunctions and disappointments, these ludicrous policies are still being repeated today.

This is all the more frustrating because some of our leaders are highly educated, and many are extremely bright. Having attended elite Western universities they come back home clutching fistfuls of certificates. There is no dearth of book knowledge or qualifications here. Yet the nation's problems only continue to intensify. So why are we still in this mess? What have these people been taught? What is the point of such qualifications if on the cold face they lead to failure?

The truth is that our leaders may be educated, but they are not savvy. They have been taught a brand of socialistic dogma that they implement unquestioningly. Instead of looking at the historic record of what clearly works and what does not, they place more faith in a misguided ideology than in their own common sense. When faced with a problem, they can only form a policy through the prism of socialistic doctrine. So time and time again we experience the same bankrupt policies being wheeled out to the ruin of our nation.

According to a famous definition, 'insanity' is a condition revealed by the habit of doing exactly the same thing repeatedly in earnest anticipation of a different result. This derangement is a pitiable condition for any sufferer, but extremely dangerous when coupled with political power. The 17th century Spanish author Baltasar Gracián once wrote, *"the sole advantage of power, is that you can do more good,"* but with unenlightened leaders at the helm, this sole advantage is squandered. It is plain to see for all, except the most blinkered observers, that such economy-wrecking measures are incredibly counterproductive and continue to have devastating effects. The inevitable result: a large underclass that finds it difficult to provide for their day to day necessities.

The welfare of our people's lives is not a joke. The symptoms of extreme poverty are profoundly serious and wide ranging. Hunger and malnutrition are the norm for families who cannot obtain enough food to sustain themselves. Children and the elderly are especially vulnerable and often suffer from malnutrition leaving them more susceptible to disease. Due to poor sanitation and medical facilities, high infant mortality rates are shamefully common.

These are areas where some targeted government intervention is essential, yet our governments prefer to divert scarce resources towards frivolous vote grabbing schemes. This results in chronic neglect in areas that would make a real difference to peoples' lives. The State wastes its scarce funds on 'anti-poverty drives' and politicians are content to make a few token gestures in the view of television cameras to give an impression of action. Only a fraction of the funds actually reach the claimed targets, the rest being absorbed in 'administration' and politically motivated allocations.

Government failures run across the whole range of indicators that measure human development. Illiteracy and ignorance ensure that the disadvantaged poor fail to build a better future for themselves. The poor are often trapped in the informal economy and so are vulnerable to those who operate outside the law. In some rural areas, the poorest practically live in servitude at the mercy of landowners. They are ignorant of their rights and their illiteracy is used against them.

It is this same vulnerability and sense of social exclusion that make the poor the most likely victims of crime and violence. As they have little access to the courts and only meagre protection from a corruptible police force, they easily fall prey to petty crime and organized criminal gangs. Inept state services, corruption and indifference are rampant at practically every level of government. Aristotle said long ago, *"poverty is the parent of revolution and crime."* He was not wrong. Due to the lack of prospects, high unemployment, rampaging inflation, and a general feeling of despair, it is no surprise that so many people must resort to illegal activities.

Throughout our history, the only effective poverty relief has mostly been of the sort provided through charitable giving. The record shows that the people of Pakistan are amongst the most generous on Earth. In situations of emergency, or even otherwise, our people can always be relied upon to place the needs of their families and neighbours above their own and to give with open hands. One of the great benefits of the Islamic way of life is that it places accountability for public relief in the hands of individuals and not the State.

The Zakat is a private act of faith, and because of this, it is highly effective in being value for money. Devout Muslims who constitute the majority of the population of Pakistan will think long and hard on where their donations are spent and why. Due to their diligence and consideration, the money is likely to go a long way. This would certainly not be the case if allocations for poverty relief were solely up to the government. Private charitable organisations play a huge role in helping the most vulnerable, however, as long as the socialistic apparatus poisons and hinders all that is potentially good in our society, only robust political action carried out to eliminate it will achieve long term, large scale results.

* * * * *

The political solution to grinding poverty is very clear and simple. There is no controversy, and there are no realistic alternatives. In order to help the poor uplift themselves in the fastest possible time, and in the most compassionate manner, socialistic notions and crude state interventions must be swiftly abandoned. The solution to poverty is the creation of a national atmosphere of economic freedom, enterprise, and dynamism where every person has a stake in the economy, and where the poor are not excluded. Encouraging rapid economic growth through the creation of wealth generating businesses will massively increase the prospects of the poorest in our society.

This can be achieved if education, health and infrastructure programmes are reformed along market lines so that they genuinely give the highest quality service to the most deserving poor. The private sector is simply more efficient, accountable and capable of delivering. Wasteful spending on ghost school buildings, chaotic hospitals, 'white elephant' projects and underused motorways should be halted. Instead, funds should be channelled to subsidize essential amenities in an efficient, free market fashion, giving those that currently go without, access to the same services that the rest of society takes for granted in the private sector.

The key to achieving this is though social mobility. Poverty decreases when social mobility increases, when the poor are able to climb the ladder of opportunity and transform their lives. This can only happen if the young and poor are offered a fair chance at achieving their aspirations. They must be given the same opportunities and resources open to the wealthy - but through private sector choice and competition. The proposals laid out in this text such as *Scholarship Voucher Schemes* and *Healthcare Accounts* go a long way in achieving this. There is no use in the State attempting to replicate what the private sector does so well and then inevitably failing in the process anyway.

Even today, most Pakistanis enthusiastically embrace the concept of the 'Welfare State'. By this they mean that the State should take a substantial role in stepping in to cure the ills of society and providing for the teeming masses directly with handouts. But the welfare state they long for is along Western socialistic lines and not the classic 'Islamic welfare state' that so gracefully provided a social safety net for the early Muslims. The Western style welfare state is the absolute last thing we would want for Pakistan. Anyone who has witnessed Western societies first hand knows full well that the practice of this system in the West has resulted in a highly permissive, demoralized and broken social structure that encourages sloth and lechery and discourages moral fortitude and hard work. The concept of welfarism has effectively mutated into *welferalism*.

Even the most staunchest advocates of this style of Western welfarism agree that it has gone too far in undermining the fabric of society, destroying family values, and creating a permanent 'feral underclass'. More often than not, the perpetuation of this system has gone far further than the originally well-intentioned social safety net concept. Moral squalor, debauchery, and social chaos is now being actively financed and propped up by politically correct, non-judgemental authorities who are effectively buying off massive swathes of their electorate schemes through bribery.

Although a social safety net is needed for Pakistan, it must be modest and tempered in its intent and practice, as was the welfarism of the early Caliphate. But more importantly, our people must finally discard their preconceived ideas that State activism can solve the problem of poverty. We have seen nothing but activism for decades. If it worked, we would have witnessed some results at least. The reality is that the State must stop hindering the escape of the masses from the clutches of poverty. The revival of self-reliance and self-confidence is the key. It is each individual, household, family and community that must actively strive and work hard to resolve their difficulties. In fact, it is already happening. It happens across our land every single day. Millions work hard, striving to provide for their families and for their future. But their path would be greatly eased if the State just got out of their way.

Because it actually achieves the required objective in the fastest possible time, what is proposed here can only be described as the most compassionate and humanitarian approach. The reason why the free enterprise system has historically worked so well in the conquest of poverty is that it is highly geared towards producing wealth. Generally in *genuine* free market economies (not ravaged by central bank instigated inflation), everyone tends to get better off, whether they are rich or poor. Increasing wealth increases the size of the national economic pie, and John F Kennedy's adage, *"a rising tide lifts all boats,"* is apt. This is provided that corruption and inflation are not allowed to act as an anchor to all but a few privileged boats.

It is time for a complete overhaul of the system. If nothing is done, then the future will only bring more of the same mediocrity and failure that characterizes the state of Pakistan today, and unfortunately, the fate of the worst off in society will only worsen. Community responsibility and individual choice is the only viable way to prevent the abuses and frustrations that we have patiently endured over the previous decades. We require a system that caters for the needs of communities, families and individuals, not beaurocrats, politicians and a myriad of vested interest groups.

Although it seems like a hopeless task, it can be done. In every advanced nation on earth, free enterprise has already conquered mass poverty. It will also do the same for Pakistan if only it is just given the chance. There is no mysterious magic formula or political mysticism involved. There is no great secret to it. Poverty can be conquered, and we know how.

16

ON ENVIRONMENT

"And this, our life, exempt from public haunt, finds
tongues in trees, books in the running brooks,
sermons in stones, and good in everything."

William Shakespeare

The world is currently undergoing a renewed surge of interest in environmental issues, and particularly issues related to carbon dioxide emissions and climate change. Although there is still much debate about the reality of global warming, it seems that Earth's atmosphere is heating up, and probably because of the activities of mankind. The world is bracing itself for the possible consequences: droughts, storms, glacial melting and desertification are already occurring with greater intensity. Ironically though, it is the people who have contributed least to the problem that may be most adversely affected - that is, the poorest of the world.

Already afflicted by poverty, corruption and underdeveloped infrastructure, the so-called 'third world' may suffer intense environmental trauma in the years to come. Yet these poor countries have only humble means to counter the effects of climate change - a phenomenon caused by the industrial rise of the developed nations, and one for which they themselves are not responsible. Having prospered on the back of reckless pollution, it is ironic to now witness these richer nations, sitting wealthy and pretty, lecturing the poor with a view to scaling back their growth and development in order to 'save the planet'.

It is a galling thing to hear. The targets of their sermons are enduring a daily struggle to survive in their fraught pursuit of life's necessities. On the very margins of survival, the world's poor use their scarce resources; food, shelter and clothing to absolute limits. Surely, never mind slamming the brakes on development, less developed nations have little choice but to continue pursuing economic growth as quickly as possible. It is the only way to uplift hundreds of millions from the curse of poverty, and it is the only humane course of action. They are not necessarily wrong in placing environmental concerns on the backburner. After all, they must first concentrate on the basic welfare of their people.

Campaigning for a better and cleaner environment and taking those to task who recklessly endanger it is an admirable and worthy pursuit. It cannot be denied though, that environmental campaigners are more likely to emerge from far-leftist, socialist backgrounds, espousing top-down government driven solutions to the problems of environmental damage. Activists tend to be highly critical of free enterprise and blame it exclusively for the problems the world faces. Considering it greedy and exploitative, activists see a profit-seeking ethos as inherently damaging and aspire to utilize the power at the disposal of the State to restrict and manipulate the market to dampen what they see as its worst 'excesses'.

We should be sceptical of any such activism that relentlessly and wrongly attacks free enterprise. Often the true agenda of such people is power - power to reshape the economic system in order to align it with their socialistic, beaurocratic needs. Heavy regulation is not the answer to preserving the environment, in fact, the evidence shows clearly that the greater the government intervention, the worse the pollution.

Command and control economies run along communist or socialistic lines are infamous for being horrendous for the environment. Examples among many include the former Soviet Union, India, Brazil, the former Soviet republics and most

African nations. These nations suffer from a malaise that is not conducive to environmental protection and tend to have the dirtiest air, the most polluted rivers, and the dreariest cities. Here the extremes of government control have been tried, and have been found wanting. It is astonishing then to witness the kind of big government thinking that is still so pervasive in activist circles. The reality is that their policies, initiatives and campaigns may be correct in their intention, but are entirely wrong in their methods.

If we were to take the words of activists at face value and look at a clear definition of their purposes, we would find much that is praiseworthy. Most visions of environmentalism see enormous benefit in clean air, water and earth. Seeking to maintain a proper balance between humanity and the rest of the natural world, they would wish to curtail man's encroachment into the last wildernesses of the world, and hope to achieve at the very least a much lower rate of species extinction. The survival of endangered species is of particular concern, as well as the reverse of undesirable pollution, greenhouse effects, global warming, and ozone depletion. Note that all of these goals are highly desirable, and there are only very few callous folk who would disagree. But presumably there is more than one way to tackle the issue, and the marshalling of State power is not the only or best solution.

But some in the ecological movement have an obvious axe to grind. Their real interest lies in the accumulation of the type of power that will help them run the lives of others, for their own good or what they perceive as the good of society. They claim that free markets are inherently evil and that the 'invisible hand' of the market is choking rather than helping. This is certainly accurate of the current state of affairs, but it need not be the case of an *environmentally just* market solution. Rest assured, we can achieve the goal of environmental preservation and protection, but only if backed by a legal and economic framework that is enabled and equipped for the task.

* * * * *

No-one can deny that in Pakistan, the environmental abuses that are taking place are of catastrophic proportions. Pollution and degradation are rife, and because of the lack of respect or even acknowledgement of the sanctity of property and life, we suffer from severe problems that will be difficult to clean up without a radical change in policy. But there is a solution. A clue to it can be garnered from the fact that most environmental problems are due in some form or another to a basic violation of *property rights*.

Oil slicks, waste disposal, air pollution, and excessive logging are mostly down to the failure of government to protect property rights either through heavy regulation, or through laws which forbid private property outright. An ideal system would take the protection and preservation of private property very seriously. Unfortunately, when sensitivity to environmental matters first made headway into the collective consciousness, the consequences were dire for private property rights. Due to being based on Western law, traditional protections of private property were, and continue to be, simply too weak to solve the underlying causes of pollution. Instead of private property rights being strengthened and developed in order to help solve the problem, they were further marginalised and replaced by draconian rules and restrictions.

The reason why government imposed 'environmental regulations' so often fail is because they lead to conflicting messages and ignore the crucial question of *incentives*. Incentives are absolutely paramount when it comes to environmental protection. It is true that government regulation and taxation can drive and guide incentives to some degree, but there are clear limits to what this kind of activity can achieve. Too often such punitive measures can often result in the exact opposite result that was intended, making a problem worse, or just moving it somewhere else.

This is par for the course for command and control economies, but under a just and sound free enterprise system, the notion that people should be able to do whatever they wish with their property, *provided* that their actions do not infringe upon the lives or property rights of others should be a basic tenet. Owners of private property have a strong incentive to protect, conserve and maintain the value of their property. They are far better stewards of resources than an unaccountable and indifferent beaurocrat could ever be. The problem with certain ecological initiatives is that they do not take this strong incentive into account.

For example, legislation that restricts the potential use of property when it is found to be of ecological or historical significance often leads to property owners to begin doing the opposite of what the law intended to encourage. If large swathes of private land are declared to be of 'special' interest to the nation, and therefore forbidden to develop on, then the value of such land quickly falls in the market. The lack of use for the land results in it being underused and poorly maintained. Unless the owner has specifically bought the land in order to preserve it through charitable funds (provided they are even allowed to), it soon falls into disrepair and turns into a burden for the property owner. By and large, what was deemed to be of special interest for the nation and hence protected under legislation thus degrades even further.

Generally, a greater breadth and depth of potential usage keeps a property valuable and sought after. It incentivises owners to look after the property and protect it from misuse. Draconian restrictions and rules will only dissuade potential owners and buyers. Given true rights over the use of their property, private owners are instilled with a strong sense of stewardship. They will act to preserve its value and will actively invest in it in order to maintain and preserve it. With freedom of action, the property becomes a valuable asset rather than a liability. This private ownership incentive should be seen as a strong ally in the struggle against environmental degradation.

But due to the inadequacy of our imported Western laws, our legal system is unable to protect private property rights to the required standard. Thus many unscrupulous characters are currently more or less excused from considering the consequences of their actions when it comes to how those actions impact on *other* property owners. When a factory emits foul fumes into the air and a nearby neighbour cannot object and demand compensation for the detrimental effects on his property, we are not seeing the legal system working as it should.

If the law is phrased in such a way as to not define the air above ones land as ones property also, but as something which is 'publicly owned', then factories will emit pollution without compunction and neighbours and passers-by will just have to suffer in silence. They may complain, but they will have to rely on the benevolence of the factory owner or the energy of a lethargic regulator, rather than through the rigour of the enforcement of their property rights through the courts.

An ideal system must allow for victims to find recourse in the court system in a way that forces polluters to bear the true cost of their pollution. Victims of pollution should be able to obtain speedy and efficient justice by filing lawsuits, making polluters pay, and obtaining court orders that prohibit future violations. But this can only happen efficiently when property rights are properly defined as to encompass all aspects of one's property - soil, air, sound etc. Only this would create an environment that was pleasant and well-maintained, on our land, in our sea, in our rivers, and in our skies.

Today, polluters in Pakistan do not 'pay' for their pollution, unless through the odd fine here or there. Should it be a surprise to us when they pollute with impunity? Legislation is rarely enforced and is highly impractical. In fact, the system is practically geared towards *encouraging* pollution. If a factory owner knows he will not be held accountable for polluting, he will simply forgo the investment that would be required to reduce the harmful pollution that his factory causes. In fact, he will lower his costs by *not* investing in clean technology, and hence become more competitive in the marketplace.

Effectively, by foregoing the cost of investing in clean technology, he will be *profiteering* from pollution. On the other hand, a socially conscious factory owner who voluntarily 'invests' in clean technology out of a high minded benevolence will suffer in the marketplace as his products and services will be more expensive and thus far less competitive. He will be driven out of the market, and his polluting competitors will prosper at his expense, resulting in a vicious cycle of pollution. It is hardly a desirable result for society.

We live under a legal regime where if a business were to be socially responsible it would put itself at a competitive disadvantage and guarantee its own bankruptcy. When property rights are not clearly defined and are not enforceable through the courts, then there is literally no way to force private (and government) polluters to bear the social cost of their operations. It is the failure of the government to uphold a legal system that protects the property rights of individuals clearly and efficiently.

* * * * *

A high growth rate and dynamic, expanding economy will lead to pressures that will inevitably impact on the environment. These pressures must be handled in a considered and thoughtful manner, not through the knee-jerk reactions of regulation and one-off fines. The best way to do this is to treat pollution as exactly what it is - *waste material*. The obligations that prevent us throwing our waste over the fence into the property next door must be applied across the board so that they encompass air, sound, water and even light.

If someone dumped their waste onto your property without your permission, you would have a legitimate right of complaint and ideally, you would have some recourse in the law. As a clear violator of your property, you could take the accused to the relevant authorities and courts and extract compensation or even criminal punishment. Even if you were highly tolerant, another neighbour might not be. Eventually someone in your neighbourhood would act. Your careless neighbour would soon realise that the proper and correct disposal of his waste is his responsibility and must be done in a way that does not violate the property rights of others. When someone's waste is invisible to the naked eye, as is the case with some forms of air and water pollution, the problem may seem more difficult to solve, but the same principle applies.

By tightening permissive property laws, not only will we give the victims of pollution access to justice, but we will also activate the power of the market to help change the behaviour of polluters in a positive manner. When victims are easily able to extract compensation, *waste material* turns into a real and transparent 'financial cost' for polluters - a cost just as real as the cost of raw materials or machinery. Because it applies to all polluters, this financial cost will be added into the total end-prices of all the goods and services in the economy in a transparent manner. Thus businesses that pollute more will have to contend with higher prices for their products in the market, de-incentivising them from polluting.

If we want to protect our environment properly and improve our standard of life as a result, it will inevitably cost money. Someone will have to pay to clean up the waste that is always produced in societies. But surely that cost must be borne by the polluters themselves in the form of higher production costs for goods and services and not by the whole of society that first suffers from pollution and is secondly forced to pay to clean it up. As long as all producers and individuals are on a level playing field as regards to being sensitive to violating other people's property with their pollution, then no polluter can gain from flouting rules and thus benefit from lower costs.

That is exactly how it should be. In this manner, only those who create waste will pay for its proper disposal, and innocent victims will no longer have to suffer. The answer lies in tougher and more transparent environmental laws that are based around the concept of private property, with proper enforcement through economic incentives, and indeed the prospect of criminal prosecution. It *is* a question of criminality. If you steal from someone else, it is a crime because you are violating their property rights, but if you knowingly pollute their air with noxious emissions, is it not a similar violation?

We should never underestimate the ability of the free market to correctly price and factor pollution in such a way as to minimise it through the transmission of signals (prices). This is exactly what the price mechanism does best. The reason why people are so sceptical about the ability of the market in these affairs is because in the environmental movement, pollution has always been considered as an *externality*. It is always treated as a tragic and unavoidable by-product of unrestricted market action rather than *internalised* into the market itself as it should be. But externalities only occur because the market malfunctions due to the inherent failings of permissive property laws. It is the failure of our government and our Western law system to maintain a system that internalises such effects into the prices of all goods and services.

In fact, robust property rights would propel the development of less environmentally damaging technologies, production methods and consumer goods. Imagine if all businesses and individuals had to pay directly for the costs they impose on others through pollution. Would it not encourage businesses to invest in technologies that minimise the environmental damage they cause? Whatever it takes to establish a competitive advantage.

The current system is broken. For one thing, we suffer from the unpleasant phenomenon of 'moral hazard'. Because pollution is not factored into the prices that end users pay, all prices are artificially low. When this happens, consumer demand will always be higher, and the hazard lies in the fact that there will be a great deal of waste and almost an incentive for people to pollute even more. For example, consumers now buy items that are very generously wrapped because they need not pay for the environmental cost of disposing the wrapping. Would they purchase as many of these items if they had to pay this cost too? Of course if this happened they would demand the item less, but then would businesses not make more profits if they devised ways to sell the same item with less damaging packaging?

The truth is that the market would needle out products and services that were most hazardous to the health of the environment because these products would be too expensive to dispose of, and consumers would thus reject them. When such prohibitive costs were passed to consumers, the demand for them would lessen if there were much cheaper (read environmentally friendly) alternatives. In effect, there would be fewer reasons to ban certain goods specifically because they are environmentally damaging. Over time, they would simply disappear from the marketplace.

Environmental damage is an injustice. Clearly, under our current Westernised laws, the problem is not being tackled. When our lives, limbs and properties are violated, there is simply no recourse through legal means to prevent abuses. The only solution is to abolish this totally inadequate legal system in favour of one which upholds property rights fully. Polluters must be held accountable and not protected by a failing system that turns a blind eye.

In his final sermon, the Holy Prophet (peace be upon him) instructed us to *"regard the life and property of every Muslim as a sacred trust."* Only a legal system which holds the lives and property of the people to be sacred can return a measure of environmental justice to our society. Only a legal system which prevents every member of society being forced to pay for the environmental crimes of a few can cleanse our nation, morally, and physically. There is only one such legal system - Shariah.

17

ON CONSTITUTIONALISM

"The two enemies of the people are criminals and government, so let us tie the second down with the chains of the constitution, so the second will not become a legalized version of the first."

Thomas Jefferson

O ver the course of this text we have laid many accusations at the door of the politicians and other assorted power-seekers who I believe have squandered repeated opportunities to change the future course of Pakistan for the better. There is no doubt that some in the upper echelons of power are corrupt and are prone to ineptitude and it is also plausible that while the status quo presides they will only continue in their current form. However, it is my belief that human weakness aside, the framework and system in which people function has a profound bearing on the depths to which individuals can sink, or indeed, the heights to which they can soar.

People function within frameworks and structures as defined by the law and by social norms, and it is the leeway the law provides that explains the degree to which individuals will take liberties beyond it. Under a restricted framework, there is less room for manoeuvre, and if the law is enforced clearly and consistently, major abuses are prevented along with most minor ones. When the law is vague, woolly, and unashamedly skewed, mal-intentioned types can potentially be highly destructive and yet still not cross the limits into illegality.

Politicians and beaurocrats working within the confines of a highly permissive law will see few limits to the extent of their activities, and thus will become energetic in their roles. At this point, whether this activity is constructive or destructive is a matter that rests at the sole discretion of the individuals in question. However, the history of Pakistan proves that if we rely on the good character and benevolence of the governing classes, then we are fools. If people have practically limitless power and there are few checks and balances on their potential actions, should we be surprised when people channel their unconfined but legal powers to oppress the people?

There are many laws and many statute books, but the most critical and dominant is the Constitution of the nation. It is the 'supreme' law of the land and it provides the very foundation of all the nation's laws. All other laws, major or minor, are only justified in their existence because they comply with its legal directives. A Constitution puts limits on the form, function and character of the State and the elected representatives who control its levers.

The need for this crucial document to hold fast against all abuses and attacks cannot be emphasised enough. When a Constitution fails, the State crosses beyond all natural limits. The resulting avalanche of lawlessness cascades throughout society, infecting everything. Because it provides the last man-made recourse to justice and accountability, a Constitution is either the last domino to fall in a free society or the first to fall in a tyranny. When it loses its essence and force and becomes a meaningless piece of paper, runaway plunder and thievery become the norm.

Whether the Supreme Court is independent or otherwise, judges must abide by the Constitution, for good or for ill. A 'supreme' law that opens the floodgates to unhindered interventionism, intrusion and immorality benefits only the elites and special interests. Such a law, bolstered by activist judges, poses a major threat to the interests of the vast majority of the people.

Since 1973, we have had just such law in Pakistan. As created by the populist socialist Prime Minister Zulfiqar Ali Bhutto, the 1973 Constitution of Pakistan comprises of the supreme law of the nation. It is claimed loudly from many corners that by living by this piece of paper, suddenly the myriad problems that Pakistan faces will suddenly wither away - ushering in a utopian era where government will act within the law and human rights will be preserved. The truth is a difficult to hear, but it must be said.

The Constitution of 1973 is seriously flawed. It is a flagrantly ideologically motivated document that opens wide all floodgates to government intervention and oppression of the common man. In spite of being a 'legal' document it is polluted with indefinable assertions, contradictions, and downright pandering. Worst of all, it gives carte blanche for all politicians to intervene in national and socio-economic life without compunction or resistance. In fact, this Constitution is so ludicrous that it has allowed the Supreme Court to authorise multiple forms of government to be conducted at its behest, ranging from social democracy to rule by military generals.

Let us be clear, the 1973 Constitution was drafted by an openly socialist leader who practiced what he preached after swaying the electorate with his populist rhetoric. When in office, his methods included extensive nationalisations (autocracy), confiscation of private property (theft), undermining of private industry (sabotage) and unchecked State intervention in the economy (tyranny) - all to the enormous detriment of the ordinary man. He has been followed by a succession of lesser or greater tin-pot dictators.

Prior to these devastating actions, the nascent Pakistani economy was poised to take-off and join the topflight ranks of the Asian tiger economies. But with Bhutto's socialism came economic catastrophe. Our fragile economy was ruined for decades to come. This is the same Constitution now placed on a mighty pedestal by the media, which after it was ratified set the optimistic course of the economy completely askew, entrenching poverty and enriching the political elites until this very day.

Every legal problem faced since then has been a direct result of our judiciary (its independence being irrelevant) holding up something as 'supreme law' which is tyrannical and socialistic in its intent and practical application. Quite frankly it is devious, and so prone to authorise all manner of evil acts, that it can only be seen as un-Islamic. Much of this Constitution is not inspired from the Holy Qur'an and the practice of the Noble Prophet (peace be upon him), but from assorted false prophets such as Karl Marx. If this is the supreme law of our land then we have been short-changed by the governing classes. Can this document be the final word for all those who seek justice and the protection of their God-given rights? Hardly. No wonder our nation has fallen so pitifully short of its enormous potential.

How far have we fallen from the straight path? Drawing 'inspiration' from the irrational and anti-God invective of communism, with a Constitution full of pandering, meaningless socialistic rhetoric and ridiculous contradictions; a document that quite frankly is not worth the paper it is written on. No surprise then, that it has been treated so shabbily by the ruling elites. The 1973 Constitution is a mere fig-leaf that is used to justify perverse and corrupt actions on the part of government. A Constitution that tolerates open-ended tyranny and neglects unalienable human rights and liberties is not what we need. This junk Constitution has not served us well and should be rethought and rewritten so as to preserve citizens rights and restrict State power rather than the reverse.

It is astonishing that in spite of the first statement of the Preamble of the Constitution stating that *"...the authority to be exercised by the people of Pakistan within the limits prescribed by Him (Almighty God) is a sacred trust...",* what follows often runs counter to commonly interpreted natural and divine law. Does the Holy Qur'an insist on the importance and protection of private property rights? Yes. The seriousness of the matter is illustrated by the relatively harsh penal code designed to deter repeated theft and robbery. So what basis is there in any virtuous law for the State to arbitrarily confiscate people's hard earned property and 'nationalise' it in order to make it public owned? Yet this is exactly what happened soon after this worthless piece of paper was ratified. Countless businesses closed and millions suffered as the State clenched its steel fist around the neck of a fragile economy.

And what is this socialistic doctrine that this Constitution legalises? It is a code of belief that hails State domination and control of resources, factors of production, and all economic life. Such a flawed system can simply not be reconciled with orthodox Islamic doctrine and law - with good reason. The material facts of history prove that such systems are not only unworkable, but result only in depravity, demoralisation and injustice.

The most legitimate economic system in the light of Islamic law is the one instated during the halcyon days of the early Caliphate, a system which operated along the principles of free enterprise, economic liberty and a sound monetary system. Coerced seizures of private property (nationalisation) are obviously unlawful, and the justification for the public or 'common' control of land, capital and property is highly dubious at best, with little or no precedent from the early Islamic era. Private property is sacrosanct, as should be the principle that the law applies to the rulers as well as those who are ruled over.

When the government has one law for itself and another for the citizens, nothing can result from this except tribulation. Our government has now been captured and is being held hostage by highly organised special interests that use it to advance their narrow objectives while imposing heavy costs on the rest of the people. It is impossible for all but a few moneyed and influential citizens to gain from such a state of affairs. The powerless masses naturally cannot compete or have the same influence in the gluttonous political arena of Islamabad. Thus they inevitably lose the game before it even begins. Yet our Constitution trumpets phrases such as fairness, social justice and egalitarianism!

This takes us to the greatest pander of all. We all know that the Holy Qur'an explicitly forbids without any shadow of a doubt the practice of 'usury'. There are countless reasons for this. Shouldn't this mean that any economic system that the Islamic Republic of Pakistan establishes should bear this in mind, and that the intention to avoid and eliminate usury should be outlined in the national Constitution? Further, should not the Constitution explicitly explain and insist on a monetary system for the nation that completely circumvents usury?

It is a reasonable assumption. Yet all we see in this vaunted Constitution is a pander. A mere sentence expressing a vague sentiment among many pages of bluster and high rhetoric stating that the state will seek to *"...eliminate riba [usury] as early as possible..." (Part 2, Article 38-f)*. No clearly defined course of action. No method by which it can be achieved. No specific timeframe indicated. And no responsibility placed on any shoulders.

Of course, there is a way in which it can be achieved, and incredibly, the non-Muslim Founding Fathers of the United States understood this. They also detested usury and the pernicious social effects of exploitative debt and interest. Being sensitive to issues of social justice, they were highly critical of inflationary and interest based fiat paper currency. They knew that such a currency would cause inflation and destroy the wealth of the poor while enriching the elite. Having personally observed the failures of the fiat 'Continental Dollar' and centralised banking systems, they were insightful enough to understand and predict that such a monetary system would lead to the kind of monetary and financial instability that we see in the form of devastating booms and busts today.

Furthermore, being fiscal conservatives, they fully understood that an un-backed paper currency which left no checks on the government's ability to print money at will, and would leave an undisciplined government to overstep all bounds in extravagance, war-mongering and oppression. They wanted to prevent future State despotism and the inevitable government inflicted pauperisation of the poor and middle classes. But they did not just espouse a mere hopeful sentiment in the United States Constitution - they had a clear, enforceable, robust solution.

The US Constitution, states in part *"...No State shall...emit bills of credit; make anything but gold and silver coin a tender in payment of debt;" (Article I, Section 10, Clause 1)*. This dates from over 200 years ago, and yet it is far superior and Islamic in spirit and action then anything the defunct constitution of Pakistan could aspire to when it comes to a monetary policy that establishes justice and integrity. The clause basically insists that dollar-value must be pegged to a gold standard. No fiat paper currencies are legally permitted and are thus unconstitutional.

Notwithstanding that since 1913 and the creation of the Federal Reserve System this clause has been ignored by the United States government, what the Founders intended was a currency that was just and sound. A currency that did not haemorrhage its value over time through inflation, and a currency that was stable, that protected wealth, and that did not allow a State Bank to fix interest rates and hence create credit-fuelled bubbles and the inevitable agonizing recessions that would follow them. Money is the single most important factor in the economy. Everyone uses it and its value affects everyone and everything. Why would we want to entrust its worth to slippery politicians and bankers?

The only way to eliminate the usury dominated economy, created with the birth of the Federal Reserve System and which then spread all over the world, is to abolish worthless fiat paper currencies like the Rupee and switch to the kind of gold and silver backed currency that was so instrumental in the fuelling of the Islamic Golden Age. By returning to the gold dinar and the silver dirham, at a stroke riba could be eliminated. The government would be forced to live within its means and become responsible to the people rather than bankrupting future generations and being in thrall to foreign powers who loan and gift Dollars and Euros with the expectation of favours that are not in the interests of the Pakistani people.

At once, the foreign boot would be taken off the necks of hundreds of millions of Pakistanis, and our country would become truly independent and sovereign. But instead what do we get in our vaunted Constitution is a vacuum of vision, dignity and integrity. Even worse, perhaps the vacuous remark about *"riba"* was probably only thrown in at the last moment to placate the 'mullahs' and 'maulvis'.

Of course, our politicians and their media shills cannot even imagine a world where their precious government and central bank does not control everyone's money, so it is no surprise that they so keenly encourage and adopt the same principles of State dominated, fractional reserve banking that are practiced internationally to the misfortune of billions of souls. For them, control over the printing presses is their stranglehold on political power.

Even a mere skimming of the United States Constitution gives rise to the certainty that although it is nowhere near perfect, it is most certainly a *legal* document, rigorous, technical and precise in its language and intent. A mere glance at the Pakistani Constitution on the other hand gives only the impression that large parts of it are simply lifted from socialist propaganda leaflets. It contains meaningless doublespeak that is so vague that a Supreme Court Judge could conceivably condone anything and everything as 'constitutional'. It is said that the definition of madness is to try the same thing repeatedly and yet expect different results. This Constitution has repeatedly failed, so why do we expect it to start working in the interests of the people now?

What is the purpose of a Constitution anyway? If we do not know, then we can never understand why our Constitution has so dramatically and continually failed to deliver. With the benefit of hindsight, historical precedent and common sense, we know that both evidence and logic prove that better government requires far less government. A virtuous Constitution that upholds and protects the rights of the people must simultaneously restrict and confine the activities of the State within set limits. A Constitution that grants open-ended powers to government rather than restricting them is one that simply invites disaster. We cannot count on the fact that our leaders will not become tyrannical.

Our constitution must through the force of law chain down *all* leaders, be they potentially benevolent or otherwise, so that human rights and liberties are always protected. We should not merely wait in hope and expectation that our future leaders will be good for the nation and not overstep acceptable boundaries. This was the beauty of the Shariah during the Caliphate. Its restrictions applied just as much to the Caliphs as to the common man. A Constitution must fetter those who come to office so that those with dark intentions are simply unable to pursue goals that contravene divine law. Thus all leaders should work within the strict limitations enumerated by Shariah which eradicate any tendencies to unchecked rule.

The best kind of law is one that clearly defines what it does *not* authorize, rather than loosely espousing what it allows - this is a hallmark of the Shariah. Thus a true Shariah-Constitution would force government to operate in just its core competencies - to establish and enforce universally applied property rights and to maximize God-gifted economic and personal liberties so that all citizens have a level playing field on which they can increase their welfare through voluntary exchange. We need a Constitution that does not allow lobbyists and special interests to use the government to pick the pockets of the people that it is supposed to protect. A Constitution that is woolly and that contains large holes, cannot be expected to prevent powerful moneyed interests from driving through spurious legislation in order to enrich themselves at the expense of all else.

A true Shariah-Constitution would not provide limitless cover for wasteful bureaucracies that only curb the choices, incentives and legitimate freedom of action of the people. Instead of fostering a corrupt government and allowing it to become a mere tool for the elites to achieve their own ends, a Shariah-Constitution would underpin the honest practice whereby all income is earned through hard work, perseverance and creativity and through the creation of useful goods and services that are actually worth more than then they cost to others.

Thus we should seek to enact a supreme law that rejects domestic subsidies and government policies that deprive honest and hardworking people of their legitimate income while restricting their choices and yet not even achieving the intended results. Although it will not be popular amongst the vampiric politicians, corporatist interests and power seekers plying their trade in Islamabad, we must finally recognize the need for a Constitution that acts in the interests of the people rather than the central government. Furthermore, we need a Constitution that treats ordinary Pakistanis like dignified, self-confident adults rather than children constantly begging their parents to give them what they want.

We must also recognise and expose the meaningless rhetoric that the governing classes use to deceive us. How many times are the words, 'freedom', 'democracy', 'the rule of law' and 'social justice' used in our defunct Constitution and how often are these same terms parroted in the media? They are the stock phrases in modern political discourse and yet the true meaning of these words is lost in the Orwellian doublespeak of politicians who are just looking after their own interests. The problem is that very few people understand the correct understanding of these words because they are so overused in the political arena they have lost all original meaning.

The writer George Orwell spoke about such abstract words and explained that they were *"often used in a consciously dishonest way"*. Certain words and stock phrases can be stacked with negative or positive associations over time. So eventually, certain meaningless phrases can be used with impunity in order to deceive and cover up unpleasant truths. So now, with its repeated parroting, the word 'democracy' has come to have highly positive associations. The word is also used extensively in the Constitution and the vast majority of people have come to believe that it is synonymous with freedom and progress, and that it is unquestionably good.

Hardly surprising, because 'democracy' is also a word that forms a cornerstone of US foreign policy. Since Woodrow Wilson espoused the intention that *"the world must be made safe for democracy,"* early on in the last century, that nation has expended enormous amounts of blood and treasure on spreading the concept and practice far and wide. Some find this obsession odd, considering that democracy is a word that is not even mentioned in the US Constitution or the Declaration of

Independence. Stranger still is the historical fact that the US founding fathers despised the notion of democracy and considered it to be something that was inherently incompatible with freedom.

They viewed it simply as 'majoritarianism', or the unchecked rule of the majority over the minority. John Adams viewed a democracy as a system where it was only the whim of the majority that granted revocable rights to minorities. He understood that the only proper system was a republic which existed to secure and protect *permanent* rights that were enjoyed by every individual, whether part of the majority or not. Our founders knew this too. Our greatest visionary leader Allama Iqbal discredited the notion with a single poetic phrase, denouncing the system as one where *"people were counted by number rather than weighed for their worth"*. This is why both the US and indeed, Pakistan, are Constitutional Republics.

We should be wary about meaningless words and phrases that are espoused by people who have something to gain. By falling hook, line and sinker for Western propaganda, we have come to give democracy a kind of quasi-religious status. We now hail it as the cure to all evils and our media constantly bleats about how free and fair elections must be held before any good can come of anything. But we have seriously misunderstood its many weaknesses and failings. Democracy is not a panacea, but merely a method of representative government, and all it has done for us thus far is to ensure the election of a series of villains, spoilers and chancers who have sabotaged the nation's future.

Rarely have elections done any real favours to the common man and yet even today, the false idol of democracy is fawned over. Our current system has failed to bring us much needed change because when people do get elected, our Constitution invests them with too much authority. If they were not power-crazed to begin with they soon become so, and all that matters then is the consolidation of more and more power. After all, there is a very fine line between governing and oppressing.

Clearly, without an underpinning of a just and fair Constitution based on the Shariah to prevent such abuses, democracy can become a tool for oppression rather than for good. We may have a Constitutional Republican system, but unfortunately we have a Constitution that is fatally flawed. It places few limits on the extent of government intervention and thus our democratically elected leaders can utilize their so-called 'mandates' to centralize power even further and amplify their misrule over the people. The result is the entrenchment of poverty, corruption, and the economic stagnation that we have endured for decades.

This appalling state of affairs is possible in spite of the pretence of constitutional oversight because our contradictory Constitution on the one hand enumerates vague citizen's freedoms and on the other hand grants open-ended State powers. Clearly, government action comes at the expense of personal political and economic liberty and vice versa. Under the present arrangement both these contrary propositions conflict with each other and result in the confusion and cover that is necessary for the subversion of the rule of law.

We must assert that Pakistan is an Islamic Constitutional Republic, and not a democracy, and we must with all haste furnish ourselves with a virtuous and progressive Constitution that establishes a very limited, decentralized government that is responsible for asserting individual economic freedoms, strong enforceable property rights and a sound monetary system that underpins an atmosphere of stability and prosperity for all. This law must protect the rights, liberties and properties of all citizens - especially from the government.

Any government action beyond these motivations including crony corporate subsidies, price fixing, heavy regulation and unfair taxation should be deemed as legally unconstitutional. The federal government must not become distracted by its unwarranted and counterproductive interventions in the economy and thus neglect its primary responsibilities of protecting individuals from illegal force, fraud and instability.

We can talk until we are blue in the face about the constitution, freedom, the rule of law and democracy but the truth is that we have no idea whether we will be truly free or not in the immediate future. One thing is for certain, the solutions to our difficult problems do not lie in our current Constitution or in surrendering our hard-won sovereignty and prostituting ourselves to the Western powers in defiance of our own national interests.

The real test is not whether we establish democratic governance with a 'pro-western' bias as many commentators salivate over and continually lecture and harangue us on, but whether the hundreds of millions of oppressed people of Pakistan can benefit from personal and economic freedom. Simply put, true and worthwhile freedom will not come with democracy as is the common belief, but with the absence of government coercion, underwritten by a Shariah-centric Constitution that enforces it. This and only this, would be a Constitution worthy of reverence and respect.

18

ON FOREIGN AID

"Why hast Thou made me born in this country, the
inhabitant of which is satisfied with being a slave?"

Allama Iqbal

When you subsidize something, you get more of it,
regardless of whether it is good or bad. It is a method of
control, and it is what the government does with certain sectors
of the economy that it wants to manipulate. But in another
sense, it is also possible for one country to subsidize another.
Through the practice of foreign aid, one nation can influence
and even control the internal practices of another very
effectively, especially if that country is relatively weaker and
poorer. It is par for the course in international relations and has
been done for thousands of years. By systematically lavishing
aid and protection, powerful nations can compel others to
surrender their inherent independence and become indentured
to a pseudo-colonial master.

This dependence is often voluntary and often there is no
military coercion involved. Quite simply, it temporarily suits the
interests of the leaders on both sides. But as Shakespeare said,
"Rich gifts wax poor when givers prove unkind." If the donors
intentions are malign, then little good comes of their aid, no
matter how generous they are. Indeed, foreign aid keeps a

recipient country on a tight leash, and by threatening to withdraw aid, or indeed withdrawing it, a master nation can extract their pound of flesh by forcing compliance on various issues that are aligned with their own interests.

Not all aid is bad. Occasionally, when there is a major natural disaster and help must be rushed to the scene, it is very helpful for neighbouring countries to contribute out of a spirit of human compassion and solidarity. But general and long term aid, designed to prop up corrupt regimes and ailing economies is far less welcome. As the case of Pakistan has aptly demonstrated, the effects can be debilitating for the recipient. Even good intentions on the part of donor nations can frequently lead to unintended bad consequences.

If only we would take tough choices and an independent line. If only we did what was right in the sole interests of our sovereignty and people. Yet it seems that the 'brown sahib' culture of servility was not eradicated after the overthrow of British rule. Unfortunately, while we wax lyrical about our independent sovereign status and take national holidays to celebrate it, we have merely replaced one colonial master with another: namely our ally, the United States. There have been no surrender ceremonies with be-medalled generals signing to and witnessing to their defeat, this surrender has come about slowly and surreptitiously.

Although America has spread its influence throughout the world, it has seen Pakistan in particular as a key nation of great strategic value. Pakistan has been seen for decades as a vital player that must be co-opted to serve American interests. America directly stations troops and bases in neighbouring countries and controls them through puppet regimes, but although it has no troops on Pakistani soil that either it or our government would admit to, our leaders cannot help but dance to the whims of puppet masters in Washington. In spite of the claimed 'alliance', American forces regularly trespass onto Pakistani territory and violates our hard won sovereignty with impunity, murdering innocent Pakistani civilians and inflaming militancy and insurgencies. But the most tragic loss for us is the loss of our self respect and dignity.

The influence of Washington casts a long shadow that stretches to the corridors of power in Islamabad. This has been achieved through tens of billions of dollars of military and economic aid gifted to successive Pakistani regimes. Our inept leadership has always welcomed these cash-laden briefcases. Following the economic failures of successive governments that have left millions mired in poverty and no effective civic society, the quality of political and moral leadership in our nation has always been inadequate. This coupled with seething ethnic tensions, wilful foreign enemies and erupting insurgencies, has led weak Pakistani leaders to cower in the shade of allies wherever they could find them.

Although 'imperially overstretched,' as America now is, there is no nation more amenable. Any excuse will do. Whether it is the spurious 'global war on terror' or 'war on drugs', our leaders are always eager to play the game. After all the profligacy, when the national treasury is spent, and no further blood can be squeezed out of the stone, there is always the line of credit that leads to Washington. Unable to govern effectively, unpopular leaders have too often extended their hands for foreign support; often only in the interests of their own personal self preservation. But no credit could be more costly.

How shameful that we should be reduced to begging and kowtowing to the same nation that mercilessly and unapologetically murders and imprisons our citizens under the guise of the so-called 'war on terror'? How much further can we fall from the dignity and honour of our illustrious forefathers? We often demand respect from others and yet we have precious little respect for ourselves. Rather than acting in an honourable, upright fashion, we prefer to strike Faustian bargains with criminals and moral degenerates who have no respect for the dignity of human life and thus kill and murder our fellow Muslims all over the world with scarcely a second thought. What would Allama Iqbal, that colossus among men, think of our present predicament? I suspect he would be gravely disappointed that we have gone so far in selling our dignity for a few measly shekels. It is about time that we recognised friend from foe.

It is important to understand that American interests in the Pakistani state are permanent and not conditional or transient. Although America claims to champion freedom, the rule of law and its brand of democratic rule, the reality is that it will support any regime that serves its purposes in maintaining its hegemony, or as its apologists put it, 'regional and international stability'. It might be useful if the Americans were more selective in the regimes they favoured. If they supported those Pakistani leaders that espoused vital reforms to improve the condition of the people it would be a good thing. But that will never happen.

The very last thing America would want is a resurgent, stable and powerful Pakistan - the Zionist elements amongst the American elite would never countenance it. Zionist policy has always been to neutralise potentially powerful Muslim nations by any means necessary, even if it means buying them off. Egypt, Saudia Arabia and Iraq are prime examples. But regardless of their intent, the fate of Pakistan surely cannot be left to depend on which direction the winds may blow in Washington, London and Tel Aviv.

Used primarily as an instrument of control and coercion, foreign aid from America and American dominated agencies such as the International Monetary Fund and the World Bank distort our national economy and prop up bad governance. Even if some of it is well-intentioned, it rarely reaches the people who need it, as it is often absorbed by many layers of bureaucracy and corrupt officialdom. When keeping oppressive governments in power, it breeds understandable resentment among the populace.

But all governments need to have sources of income. Government expenditures financed by interest based loans or the printing presses merely distort the economy and create insidious inflation. The only truly legitimate source of State revenue is taxation. This makes the government accountable to the people and the people alone. When it accepts foreign aid, the government displaces its priority of serving the people with gratitude to the generous donor. But what if the interests of the donor and the people do not coincide? Looking at our history, leaders with a sense of national loyalty and patriotism have been few and far between. No cynicism here, just reality. More often than not, when interests clash, the regime will naturally tend to favour its foreign benefactor.

Excessive State spending of any kind is inadvisable if the government is to stay small and limited and if free enterprise is to be allowed to flourish. Potential funds that come from a foreign source are spent in the national economy via the State, and good or bad, they only increase the presence of the State in the economy. When these funds are spent, they often come with caveats. These conditions mean that they cannot be spent where they are actually needed. A beaurocracy under the guise of 'checks and balances' leads to much of the expenditure being channelled through contracts with the donor nations own organisations. So in reality, foreign aid is sometimes merely an opaque mechanism for a donor nation to subsidise and support its own domestic companies and interests operating abroad. What use is such aid?

It is time to face facts. Pakistan has received aid to the tune of many billions of dollars from many countries since its creation. Can anyone reasonably argue that this has materially benefited the majority of the people? It is only good governance that matters, and this is why the blame lies with us. We have failed to govern ourselves properly and have thus had to resort to prostituting our sovereignty to foreign nations who only wish to subjugate us and prevent our ascendance. This foreign 'assistance' has done incalculable harm, fortifying an elite class in power who wallow shamelessly in corruption and high treason.

Charity and aid from foreign private individuals and organisations is fine, but aid from other governments should be politely refused. Often the excuse is made that the country is strapped of money and investment. But that pitiful excuse is solely down to the socialist and interventionist tendencies of the regimes in power. With a failed State education system, a harsh business climate, and a maze-like bureaucratic process, there is little wonder that people fail to see the rewards of investing in our country. There are too few rewards in doing so.

Foreign aid is often billed as a catalyst to jumpstart economic development. But that is equally ridiculous. Only sound economic policies can do such a thing. Any government that liberalised and deregulated the economy, set its entrepreneurs free, and lowered taxes would naturally attract much more in foreign private investment than any foreign donor could possibly send in assistance packages.

Foreign aid does not create prosperity but distorts internal markets and props up inefficient companies and corrupt elites. It is a great tool for foreign governments to buy political allegiances and sway policies, but it does little or nothing for the people. It is time for us to abandon this ludicrous inferiority complex and re-declare our independence. Pakistan is an Islamic Republic. We place our trust solely in Allah. He is enough for us.

* * * * *

We need trade, not aid. The only way to break free of international dependencies is to become prosperous through domestic entrepreneurship and global commerce. Weak and poor countries can be easily manipulated, but wealthy countries can afford to navigate an independent course in international matters. With the increasing globalisation of the world economy, it is easier than ever to exploit lucrative foreign markets and benefit from high quality foreign imports. Our interaction with the international community should not be on the basis of us being a grateful recipient of aid, but as an equal participant in international trade and investment. By trading freely with other nations to mutual advantage, we can enrich ourselves far more than any aid could benefit us.

By locking into an increasingly globalised world in order to trade and exchange with others, we do not surrender our national sovereignty. Instead, we actively empower our people and our nation. Whereas aid primarily benefits the elite through whose hands the funds flow, international trade benefits the ordinary man. With cheap imported goods accessible to the people and more acute competition to sharpen the quality of our domestic industries, there are very few losers under a free trade regime. Productivity, employment and innovation is significantly boosted, as is the rapid growth of sectors of the economy in which we have a clear comparative advantage. We should not wish to insulate our domestic industries from foreign competition, but instead expose them to new ideas, products, technologies and innovations. Some will fail, but the best will survive and join the ranks of global brands and marques. Autarky and self-sufficiency is a foolish and ignorant policy objective. The Pakistani people should benefit from a wide array of accessible consumer goods from all over the world. Lower prices and cut-throat competition for their business will improve the living standards of millions of our poorest compatriots.

It is very important that we distinguish between the free trade that brings the most benefit and the so-called 'managed-trade' regimes that only benefit a few corporate elites who have the ear of the administration in power. Trade organisations such as the WTO are only instruments that foreign governments use to control the flow of trade in a fashion that will benefit their own favoured domestic companies. It is not free trade or anything of the sort, but is simply a form of blatant protectionism that is disguised through the language of free enterprise. Such organisations should be avoided, as there is no benefit to membership. Trade organisations, agreements and delegations are simply a waste of time and money. Such negotiations and bilateral agreements result in less trade rather than more. They only provide an excuse for politicians and bureaucrats to go on extravagant foreign excursions at taxpayers expense.

There is only one way that international trade should be conducted, and it involves a single unilateral step. History and economic science have demonstrated that the best possible course of action for a country is to abolish tariffs and barriers when it comes to international trade. This is always beneficial, regardless of whether neighbouring countries pursue protectionist policies or not. By unilaterally declaring a free trade regime, Pakistan can reap the enormous rewards of increased prosperity, productivity and growth. We do not need to seek permission or authorisation from any foreign country or global trade organisation and neither do we need to painfully negotiate for years on end to sign bilateral agreements that will only benefit corporatist elites. We simply need to abolish our tariffs. There will be initial pains to some, but the overall good that will come as a result will be overwhelming.

It has become fashionable recently to espouse views that poverty in the third-world is due to a lack of so-called 'fair-trade'. This is only yet another example of economic illiteracy. Quite simply, it is the lack of any trade at all that causes poverty. Any barrier to trade that comes in the form of 'managed' exchange and that sets high criteria on participants or excludes others only restricts the ability of the very poorest to escape poverty. Free trade saves lives. It's as simple as that.

The solution is to become an equal participant in the new globalised economy and to strive and compete. Instead of relying on handouts from other nations that would seek to exploit us, we should open our eyes and reflect on our situation. Contrary to popular global opinion, Pakistan is no mere banana republic. We are a nation of nearly 200 million people, with an abundance of natural resources and a deep pool of ambition and enterprise. We are destined for leadership of the Ummah if not the whole world. We should be blazing a trail for ourselves into a bright and prosperous future.

Clearly, no amount of aid or assistance from anyone will replace the fact that Pakistani leaders have failed to govern the country in a moral and competent manner. It is essential that we take the necessary reforms and actions that are needed to unleash the creative energies of the people. Pakistan needs to return to sound money, limited government and free enterprise. This will provide us with the fastest route to economic and social development. This is the only way that we can turn tail from being a dependent recipient to one day soon becoming a benevolent donor.

19

MY VISION

"It's not what you look at that matters, it's what you see."

Henry David Thoreau

The will of the Almighty applies everywhere. Not a leaf falls from a tree nor an atom moves from its place unless Allah permits it. How quickly we forget the natural inherent laws that govern His creation. It only requires a little thought and reflection to realise that there is beauty and elegance in even the most obscure of places. Granted, there is enormous splendour in a mountain landscape, grace in the flight of a bird, and inspiration in the vast starlit sky, but do we ever think of the marvel whereby two human beings can come together in the spirit of commerce, with only their self interest at heart, and yet both benefit from the exchange?

Is it not miraculous the manner in which prices regulate and adjust themselves naturally in the marketplace, accommodating both demand and supply? Not guided or regulated by any hand, but merely through natural occurrence? How is it that even something as lowly as a mere pencil is formed through the work and insight of thousands of different and disparate people, all of whom contributed and collaborated in its manufacture in their self interest, and yet to the benefit of society too?

Why can we not recognise these profound truths, and why do we deny and dismiss these miraculous processes by ignorantly claiming them to be exploitative and evil? In reality, they govern the world in which we live, and they would be enormously beneficial to us if only we would let them do their work. The inherent ingenuity of the free market supplies all demands while providing demand for all supply. Through the natural movement of prices, wages, rents and capital returns, the whole of mankind's economic existence is stabilised. Countless differing decisions, preferences, wants and wishes are thus maintained and catered to. No government machine can replace this awe inspiring natural balance.

On the Day of Judgement, no group or government will be held to account, rather, it is we that will be held accountable as individuals. For all the talk of collectivism, we have lost sight of the bare fact that we cannot lose our own individual nature in the ether of the collectivist world-view. The Almighty has gifted all of us, every one of us, with a free personality. We accepted this burden freely, and we now exercise this liberty at our own peril. On that Day, there will be no shelter in collectives and no shade in any government from the scrutiny of the Final Judgment.

We hold our destiny in our hands. We must utilise our abilities to better ourselves, our families, our communities and our beloved nation, all while 'holding fast to the rope of Allah'. We were created to worship and depend on the Almighty alone, and no other. This is our creed: *there is no God but Allah, and Muhammad is His messenger.* We place our trust in Him and Him alone. He suffices for us. No State, faction or party can replace His mercy and provision.

Once we recognise ourselves, and our purpose, we can recognise the purpose of our government. It exists to uphold divine justice, protect the welfare of the weak, guarantee law and order, ensure the integrity of the currency, and protect the nation from foreign aggression. It is not meant to place people in distress and become a means for a privileged few to plunder and oppress the rest. Its purpose is to provide all citizens with the stability and space to reach their potential.

The government must serve, and not be served by the people, and every capable person must utilise their creative faculties to grow and prosper, spiritually and materially. Being accountable for our individual actions, we must do our best to personally fulfil our obligations to each other, and we must not rely on or expect the government to be a remote caretaker that supplants our own sacred responsibilities to our families and neighbours. On the Day of Reckoning, will it be of any use to say that we failed to help others in their time of need because we expected the government to?

Liberty and Islamic practice are two sides of the same coin. Neither can function optimally without the other. Only with freedom can we practice our faith, and only with faith can we temper our freedom. In a predominantly Muslim society like Pakistan, the widespread adoption of sound orthodox Islamic practices, all ascribed to on a voluntary basis, provide the best framework of natural social regulation, creating harmony, peace, and tempering people's worst excesses.

If we wish to establish true social justice we must create an environment where people 'do not regulate and oppress others for their own benefit, but instead regulate themselves for the benefit of others'. Our salvation does not lie in government coercion - it lies in Islam, a path of truth, especially if not sabotaged by a misguided leadership that indulges in immorality.

Unfortunately, in our mindless adoption of socialism, we have forgotten and marginalised our finest values. Yet even now, the proponents of so-called 'Islamic socialism' still try and claim the moral high ground. Many believe that economic freedom is undesirable because it is exploitative, degenerate and leads to social inequality. This outlook is baseless, but it is often parroted by propagandists who remain enslaved to these fashionable yet misguided beliefs. The claim free enterprise promotes greed. But greed has nothing to do with the classical Islamic model we wish to revive. Here, one invests, saves, risks and works hard for ones living; yet today under so-called 'Islamic socialism', one has a sense of false entitlement and expects all others to be forced to pay for ones way. Which system really encourages greed?

We need to understand once and for all that free enterprise does not degrade moral values or lead to social injustices. Free enterprise is economic freedom, and as such, it is inherently Islamic. It was the economic model that was established in Muslim lands during the halcyon era of the Islamic 'Golden Age'. The record is clear. In a Muslim society that is sovereign and independent, and where the State abides by divine law and does not arbitrarily confine or restrict liberty, Islamic sentiments and values will flourish. Righteousness will flourish. Prosperity will flourish. When we follow the will of Allah, how can it not? Why would we call it our 'Golden Age' if it this were not true?

Many of the misguided amongst us would love to embrace the West in all its totality and indeed, some already do. They yearn for the *westernisation* of Pakistan. But this is the last thing we would want. Fortunately, free enterprise will not result in the decadent *westernisation* that we all fear, it will lead to *modernisation*. This is exactly what we need - a shift to modernity, prosperity, science and high technology. We do not need to import the worst of Western values. We intend to develop our own values and culture on our own terms, but with the trappings of modernity too. Tragically, so far, all we have endured is *westernisation* though the import of 'scientific socialism.'

Even though some apologists still have the gall to call it 'Islamic', it is this creed that has degraded our moral values. We only need to look at the state of our society and others like it for proof. When an expanding State gets bigger and bigger and encroaches more and more into every aspect of human life, it becomes jealous of the divided loyalties and sense of independence that religion and spirituality engenders. Repeatedly in history, socialistic and fascistic states who tried to direct all life on a 'scientific' basis, all sought to marginalise faith and spiritual activity, systematically attempting to replace it with complete obedience and trust in the State itself.

Now we hear the same talk in Pakistan that was heard in the West not so long ago. That faith 'should be relegated to the private sphere', that there should be a 'separation of church and State'. The Western world is now demoralised and spiritually broken. Its people have no sense of purpose. Do we want the same fate for ourselves? As ethics become *relativistic,* and social norms and moral codes are changed at the whim of the governing classes, social breakdown is inevitable. When politicians go so far as to dictate all human activity in detail, trying to mould and fashion it in their self-interest, morality and justice is always compromised. Let us beware. It is no coincidence that the 'intelligentsia' who rule over us are so contemptuous of Islamic values.

There is no doubt in my mind that socialism has greatly hindered the spread of true Islam - instilling a sense of dependency and misplaced faith in the government by the masses. Its profound social, economic and cultural failures have postponed our spiritual and material progress and given root to desperate religious and political extremism - even insurgency and terrorism. The economic stagnation and weakness that has resulted has left Pakistan vulnerable to the canny manipulations of foreign powers. No one can deny that we are not a free and independent nation. Our sovereignty is an illusion. Our fate and leadership lies in the hands of foreign governments and puppet-masters who can make our leaders dance to their tune.

We may pretend that this is not true, but we would be deluding ourselves. Our fiat currency is increasingly worthless, our military is forced to counter domestic insurgencies, our police are disillusioned and demoralised, our schools are failing our children, our hospitals are crumbling and inaccessible, our central bank is fuelling the inflation that is destroying what little wealth our people have left, our society is becoming increasingly fractured along ethnic and regional lines, our borders are unprotected, our reputation lies muddied, our politicians are crude opportunists without vision and insight and it would seem to the average observer that our future seems none too bright.

Not so.

True enough, mediocrity, moral corruption, and aimlessness have embedded themselves into the composition of our nation. The damage has been incalculable. True enough, we are facing a vast coterie of vested special interests who will not give up their grip on power easily. They will resist reform and try to defend their interests using whatever means they can muster. True enough - but all is not lost. Time is slipping away, and so is our beloved country, but if we act now, we can right ourselves quicker than anyone can imagine. We just need the courage to do so. It will be difficult, but it is possible. In fact, I believe it is inevitable.

Most people know what the problems that the nation faces are. They endure them and are witness to them on a daily basis. What they are unaware of is the causes of these problems, because such analysis requires a deeper understanding and insight than most people have. In the streets and homes where friends and family gather, the conversation often turns to the lambasting of the political system and the politicians who infest it. But when potential solutions are offered, they always seem to involve the government yet again: with a different stripe of politician perhaps, with more regulation, more government programs, and yet more government expenditures. Because they do not understand that it is primarily the government that has fostered and exacerbated their troubles, and because the government has encouraged the belief that only it can provide the solution, most people still look to the same government as the potential saviour.

This is very serious. The failure to correctly diagnose the causes of an illness can only postpone the cure. It is a cause of great frustration because in order for Pakistan to finally make progress and for us to create a robust consensus on what is to be done, it is a fallacy that must be vigorously countered. The people must be illuminated with the truth. Part of the problem is that this fallacy is deep-set in the hearts and minds of the educated chattering classes and liberal media. When even the elite classes, political cheerleaders and leading opinion makers have themselves bought into the fallacy of big government and so-called 'social democracy', it is no surprise that Pakistan's economic performance has been so disappointing.

While such unfounded viewpoints are so commonplace, it is unlikely that Pakistan can ever break the cycle of its own self destruction. That is why we must change these views. There is hope if only we educate and illuminate the masses through articulate persuasion and reasoning. Understanding and empathising with people's daily troubles, we must offer the solutions that have proven to be the only ones that work when we take into account our own history and the accumulated economic knowledge and experiences of other nations.

Once and for all, we must convince the masses that socialistic governance is a force that stunts growth and impedes our progress, a force that is holding back our nation from a great destiny. We must realise that under our existing system, the entrenched political elite have no interest in securing the legitimate rights of the people. They know that when the people finally do secure their rights, their liberation will come at the expense of those in power. After all, being part of the status quo, the consolidation of their positions is their paramount concern.

For far too long our nation's leaders have hustled their way into power, with too few reasons for doing so. For most, all that matters is how they will get into the chair, and how they will keep it. The question of 'why' never occurs to them. The media gushes with their latest ramblings on democracy, human rights, extremism, and military dictatorship. The hue and cry is always about who is in power, and who is trying to get there - never about why they deserve it. We are told ad nauseam about the antics of the power-mongers, but we never question the word 'power' itself, or what it entails. People see the acquisition of power as perfectly natural. But why should it be?

So many of Pakistan's problems have resulted from political figures who fanatically and ruthlessly sought the accumulation of power, only then to wield that power recklessly, with no due regard or respect for any law, natural or divine. It cannot come to us as a surprise. Our flawed constitution is used both as a shield and a sword for such characters to get their way. They both defend their actions and justify their aggressions through it, using it as a mere tool of political cover. A supreme law that truly protected the interests of the people would never allow such latitude on the part of the holders of high office.

A worthy constitution would acknowledge that prosperity and peace comes easily if liberty, sound money and the rule of law for all is guaranteed. It would be a document that chains down the power of the politicians, and protects the rights of the people by restricting the potential destructive actions of their government.

We must try and strive towards a kind of government where political power is markedly reduced. The kind of government where those who hold high offices of State, do not hold such high status. With less power to wield, they would be less likely to be surrounded by flunkies, cronies and special interests, currying favours at the people's expense. With limited government, Shariah law and a sound currency, their ability to tax, spend, borrow and regulate would be curtailed, and there would be no threat of misguided activity.

Unrestrained power, not subject to any law or limit, acts as a poison - a fatal concoction of deceit, treachery and greed that infiltrates through all society. It has destroyed the rule of law, aggravated mass poverty, and compromised our hard-won, hard-defended freedoms. Yet such political power is still glorified. Until we learn that power is something to be treated with caution, and something which should not be placed on a high pedestal, we will be lost. Most of all, in the hurly burly of politicking in Islamabad, we need more vision, more humanity and more hope. We need leaders who instead of falling over themselves to tell us what we want to hear, tell us what we badly need to know.

We must strive for the kind of leadership that will bring genuine change; a leadership that will pledge to restore the Islamic free enterprise model of our forefathers. If our nation is to ascend from the ashes, new leaders must arise. We need an honest, thoughtful and courageous band who like Iqbal and Jinnah, can maintain an independence of mind and spirit, and who recognise the futility of making idols of Western ideas.

Most of our fellow countrymen and women want to flourish, develop and live better than their forefathers; they want Pakistan to live up to the destiny that our founders envisioned. They have great pride in their beloved country and want to see it become a beacon of light and progress in the Islamic world. So far, they have been disappointed, Of course, the doomsayers say there is no use, that we should resign ourselves and surrender to our pitiable fate. Let them spew their cynicism - they are on the wrong side of history.

In 1930, at a public address, our leader Allama Iqbal spoke these profound words: *"...Muslims must prepare for independent and concerted political action. At critical moments in their history, it is Islam that has saved Muslims and not vice versa. If today you focus your vision on Islam and seek inspiration from the ever vitalizing idea embodied in it, you will be only reassembling your scattered forces, regaining your lost integrity, and thereby saving yourself from total destruction."* His voice echoes through the generations, but he could have said these words just yesterday.

My fellow countrymen, it is time to arise and awake. Imagine and understand what a truly great nation Pakistan could become. We need to understand ourselves so that we can understand what must be done. So far it seems that only the grace of Allah has protected Pakistan through its successive breakdowns and crises, but we must become those that Allah helps because they *'first help themselves'*. We must take responsibility for our own country rather than continually delegating it to the most unscrupulous and ruthless among us. Are our sights set too high? Are we deluding ourselves? Are our people too divided? Is our country broken beyond repair?

Not at all.

One day, and one day soon, the people of Pakistan will gather around under a common purpose. Striving in a manner that exemplifies all that is best in the spirit of mankind, we will achieve that great destiny that the cynics have called a delusion. We will achieve that great destiny that inspired our visionary founders, but which only few of us dare to dream of any more. When Pakistanis of every stripe - Balochis, Sindhis, Punjabis,

Pashtoons, Kashmiris all; whether rich, poor, young or old, finally stand up and proclaim that we are one nation, one Ummah, with one Prophet, and One Allah, and our time has come.

We will reject the chicanery and pettiness that has consumed Islamabad; we will remove power from the hands of the power crazed elites, and place it back in the hands of the deserving masses that have suffered for so long. We will stop bickering and fighting amongst ourselves, and in the spirit of freedom and brotherhood, we will finally appeal to the better angels of our nature. On that great day, we will finally meet and overcome the complex challenges that face us as a people.

Choosing hope over cynicism and unity over division, we will seize our country back from the unscrupulous power-mongers that have plagued us. No longer will special interests, lobbyists, and cronies dictate the fate of tens of millions and plunder our country with impunity. No longer will foreign powers hold our entire nation hostage to their selfish whims and interests, and no more will the injustices that have trampled over the hopes and dreams of so many be allowed to continue unchecked. We will enjoy the governorship of leaders whose powers are deployed with wisdom and who are honest and sincere. We *can* achieve this.

By organising ourselves, and bracing ourselves for the battle ahead and fighting and striving to make the lives of millions better, we *will* re-establish the dignity, honour and respect of not just Pakistan, but the entire Ummah. Picture it: a 'Federation of Islamic States', each autonomous, but all united, each sovereign, but all inter-dependent. More than a billion Muslims, all bound together in common purpose, resolute in defending each other, compassionate in caring for each other.

A haven of peace and calm for all humanity, stretching from the Pacific to the Atlantic. No longer will the followers of the Noble Prophet (peace be upon him) be subject to terror and evil at the hands of oppressors. Yes, there will be setbacks, even pitfalls, but even the most arduous tasks are not difficult to achieve by pious people who instilled with a sense of purpose, and in spite of the great odds stacked against them, work and strive for change out of the love and devotion they have for Allah and His Messenger (peace be upon him).

This is not blind optimism. Considering our great qualities, our strengths, our ingenuity and national spirit, it is rational, calculated and achievable. The tasks and challenges ahead are vast but they are certainly not insurmountable. We cannot and must not shirk from the battle before us, because we know with certainty and faith that something better lies around the corner. Something that will improve the lives of countless millions, if only we would reach for it, strive for it, fight for it.

We must tear down the barriers that the politicians and beaurocrats have erected to confine and control us, and instead of resorting to the factional politics that chain people down, we must lift our people up. By freeing individuals, families and communities - house by house, street by street, city by city, province by province, we can demonstrate that where government fails, ordinary people can achieve extraordinary things for their country.

What awesome potential we have! With our population, resources, ingenuity and vision, we could become a superpower within a few short years. We could become the glittering hope of the Muslim world, a source of inspiration and emulation - the greatest nation in the history of the earth. We could reclaim the mantle of Islamic civilisation and raise our banner high and defend it with honour. We could regain the respect of the world.

We could do all of these things, and much more besides, if only we are ready to take our country in a fundamentally new and hopeful direction. These are not false hopes. They are not pipe dreams. They are real and achievable intentions. A chorus of cynics will tell us loudly and arrogantly that we cannot do it. Yes, no doubt, the battle ahead will be treacherous, but what force on Earth can stand in the way of millions of voices calling for change?

We can do this. We have hope.

The same hope that filled the hearts and minds of those visionary leaders who first contemplated and strove for partition and independence even against impossible odds.

The same hope that lead to the creation of Pakistan on a Night of Power during a holy month of Ramadan - the emergence of the world's first true Islamic republic, a Land of the Pure, a new Medina-e-Sani, a nation destined for honour and greatness.

The same hope that drove millions upon millions to strike out from their homes and hazard the agonies and risks of crossing the border to the Promised Land.

The same hope that remained in those brave migrants hearts, even as their defenceless friends, family members and neighbours were martyred in cold blood - massacred by barbarians and savages.

The same hope that enabled generations of brave patriots to defend their beloved homeland time and time again, on land, sea and air from intimidation, violent aggression, and the threat of annihilation.

The same hope that even today, after all the disappointments and broken promises, still remains in the hearts of hundreds of millions who just want a better life, a better future, and a better nation for their children.

And all along we have been told that we cannot do it, that we face insurmountable odds - that we should not even bother to try. But we have faced such trials before - far greater trials. By all accounts, we should not even be here.

We still are.

We are the people of Pakistan. We are one people, and we are one nation. Our faith is Islam, our identity is Pakistani. Together, we can begin a new era in our nation's history. Together, we can overcome. We can come out of the long darkness and achieve wonders and glories beyond our wildest imaginations. We can have opportunity and prosperity. We can repair our society. We can heal our nation. We *can* fulfil our manifest destiny.

And we will.

20

CALL TO ACTION

They say that it can't be done. They say that change will never come. They say that our beloved country is broken. They say that there is too little hope. They say that it is too hard. They say our people do not care enough. They say that *no one* cares enough.

They are wrong.

It is too easy to be dismissive, disillusioned and disenchanted and to enter the conclusion that the vested interests and governing classes are too powerful, and that change is impossible.

Our leaders have dealt fatal blows to our economy, to our people, to our dreams, to our hopes and, to our reputation and honour around the world.

They have injected a sense of fatalism into the psyche of the people, creating an intellectual and spiritual despair that breeds extremism, a conspiratorial mentality and widespread ignorance.

Poverty is epidemic, inflation is out of control and political and corporatist corruption is rampant. We are in a crisis that our visionary founders could never have imagined. We *need* change now, more than ever before.

Let me tell you something that I fervently believe - and it is because I believe it, that I wrote this book. If we have the necessary courage, hope, faith and determination, we *can* solve our problems.

Faith is what we must cling to. Faith in Allah, faith in each other, and faith in our manifest destiny. We have been wronged, we deserve better, but only we can make the changes that we look for others to make.

We have diagnosed our problems, and we know the cure to our ills. We just need to take the next step. Together, we can unleash a bright future, full of hope and aspiration, where we cast aside our fears, uncertainties and doubts, and make not just our country, but our whole world a better place.

We are sent to this earth for a reason. To be righteous, worship Allah, and to leave this Earth a little better than when we came to it. How many of us can claim that we are fulfilling our responsibilities?

Some of us have been greatly blessed. Blessed with talent, prosperity and prospects. We are blessed with the kind of lifestyles of ease and security that are out of reach of the vast majority of the people. I know I am. Well, to whom much is given, much is expected.

We must face up to our responsibilities. We need to work hard and persevere in spreading a powerful message that will bring the changes that will ensure that more and more people benefit from freedom, prosperity and dignity.

We need not tolerate indifference and incompetence from a government that is prostituted to special interests and foreign powers. Not anymore.

Let's be clear. Such sweeping changes are not realistically possible through the sole efforts of the grassroots. Talking from the sidelines is cheap, and the only way to effect real change is through the *struggle for high political office*. Time is quickly running out for Pakistan. We need to eject an entire generation of spineless Islamabad politicians from the corridors of power.

They have failed. No more chances.

We need a new generation of politicians. The message is easy to understand, and it is popular. It simply needs to be transmitted to the masses. We need leaders who enjoy passionate, mass popular support to be united under a common patriotic cause with a clear vision for the future of Pakistan. Could you be a leader? Why not?

The entrenched establishment will be wise not to stand in our way. We need a new kind of politics in Islamabad. We need politicians in office who will turn it from a city of comfort and relief for elites into a city of despair for them. Why? Because, in the despair of the socialists and inflationary capitalists, lies the hope of our beloved Pakistan.

Right now all we have are power-seekers and pseudo-intellectuals who are as we speak, priming for further expansions of federal power, writing yet more pointless regulations, exponentially increasing corporate subsidies and welfare, printing money like confetti, creating more havoc and extremism in independent minded regions of the country, and worst of all, finding new ways to humiliate the poor mortals who only try to live decent, honest and law-abiding lives.

We must have people striving for political office, who are dedicated to resurrecting the fallen remains of Islamic civilisation and giving it new life, breath and dignity. Take up the cause. You know what needs to be done.

The plans we have are pioneering, visionary and eminently humane. Smaller government, economic freedom and sound money. These ideas may seem reactionary, but they are only a return to our glorious heritage. I believe, and it has been foretold by our betters, that our civilisations greatest days do not lie behind us, but in front of us.

The Holy Qur'an does not sanction or authorise socialism or inflationary capitalism. It is these ideologies that are immoral, discredited and reactionary. We need to rid ourselves of its shackles and set our people free.

Dear reader, you have the most important part to play. Absorb this message. Reflect on it. Understand it. And spread it. To everyone you can, in whatever way you can. If you, like me, are sick and tired of the status quo, then let us take a stand together. If not now, then when? How bad do things have to get before we act?

No. Enough is enough. The stakes are far too high, and the cost of failure is already being felt in the pain and anguish of our people. But there is hope. Change will come. And we will be victorious. If we have faith, then we can prevail for the sake of Allah.

So with Allah as our witness, let it not be said that no one cared, that no one objected, that no one spoke out. May Allah have mercy on us all, and may He bless our Muslim brothers and sisters and our beloved Pakistan forevermore. Ameen.

Pakistan Zindabad.

NOTE

O ver the years I have read many books by Pakistani and other thinkers which have been unsatisfactory in their analysis and diagnosis of Pakistan's unique issues.

What I have crudely attempted here is to posit solutions to Pakistan's myriad problems in a spirit of empathy and genuine concern. In the process I have tried to be as detailed as I could hazard to be, and at risk of becoming a hostage to fortune, I have posited solutions that I believe would go a long way in solving these complex problems.

This text should not be read as a political manifesto. It is not one, although it is perhaps a step in that direction. It is my commentary and analysis on the situation in Pakistan, and should be seen in that light.

You will note that there are no references or notes provided, and this is deliberate, as I felt that the fluidity of the text would not be served by such footnotes. This is not to say that everything in this text is original, as it certainly is not.

The ideas espoused in this text have been developed over many years and after a great deal of research and deliberation, and I fully acknowledge that much of the contents are based on the writings and ideas of many esteemed intellectuals and thinkers of historical note, too many to mention without doing injustice to those omitted.

Truth prevails over falsehood. Any mistakes in this text are my own, and any good that comes from it, is from Allah.

AUTHOR

Atif F Qureshi was born in Benghazi, Libya in 1982. He is a writer and entrepreneur. He maintains an active blog at his website *www.pakdestiny.net*, with ongoing commentary on the current political and economic situation in Pakistan.

* 9 7 8 0 9 5 5 6 5 7 0 0 9 *